Three Treatises
ON THE NATURE OF SCIENCE

GALEN

Three Treatises
ON THE NATURE OF SCIENCE

On the Sects for Beginners
An Outline of Empiricism
On Medical Experience

Translated by
RICHARD WALZER and MICHAEL FREDE

with an Introduction by
MICHAEL FREDE

Hackett Publishing Company

GALEN: A.D. 129–ca. 200

Cover design by Richard L. Listenberger
Interior design by Baskerville Book & Editorial Services Company

For further information, please address

Hackett Publishing Company
P.O. Box 44937
Indianapolis, Indiana 46204

Library of Congress Cataloging in Publication Data

Galen.
   Three treatises on the nature of science.

   Bibliography: p.
   Includes index.
   Contents: On the sects for beginners — An outline of
empiricism — On medical experience.
   1. Medicine, Greek and Roman—Addresses, essays,
lectures.   2. Medicine—Philosophy—Addresses, essays,
lectures.   3. Medicine, Empirical—Addresses, essays,
lectures.   I. Title.
R126.G3923   1984   610   84-19826
ISBN 0-915145-91-X
ISBN 0-915145-92-8 (pbk.)

Contents

Introduction   ix

Bibliography   xxxv

On the Sects for Beginners   1

An Outline of Empiricism   21

On Medical Experience   47

Index of the Persons
Mentioned in the Texts   109

Index of the Subjects
Mentioned in the Texts   111

Three Treatises
ON THE NATURE OF SCIENCE

Introduction

This volume contains translations of three treatises by Galen which introduce us to a philosophical debate among Hellenistic doctors which has
not received the attention it seems to deserve. This debate, which arose
towards the middle of the third century B.C., concerns first of all the
nature of medical knowledge. But though the debate also addresses questions which arise due to the specific nature of medical knowledge, what is
at issue for the most part is the nature of expert or scientific knowledge
quite generally, even if this issue is discussed almost exclusively in terms
of medicine. It was in this debate that, for the first time, a sharp and clear
contrast was developed between rationalism and empiricism. In fact, the
very terms *empiricist* and *rationalist* have their origin in this debate. The
dispute divided the medical profession so much that it fell into two war-
ring camps, whose partisans came to be called "Rationalists" and
"Empiricists". Both groups proceeded to articulate and refine their
respective positions in great detail and to attack their opponents with
considerable verve and ingenuity. But neither side saw reason to yield.
Those on each side seemed to have developed a sufficiently stable and
coherent position, from which they were able to answer the objections of
their opponents. Thus the dispute threatened to become rather barren
and somewhat academic. And this all the more so since, at least to Galen,
it seemed that both sides agreed as to how patients were to be treated
and disagreed only as to how the right treatment had been discovered, by
experience or on the basis of some scientific theory. Hence it was only
natural that, after more than two centuries of debate, some doctors
should try to look for a way out of this stalemate by trying to find a position which would be immune to what seemed to be justified empiricist
criticisms of rationalism and also to what seemed to be equally justified
rationalist criticisms of empiricism. Such a position the so-called Methodists claimed to have found. Thus, from the first century A.D. onwards,

the debate became a three-cornered dispute among Rationalists, Empiricists, and Methodists, which died out only in the course of the third century A.D.

In spite of its great importance and interest, not much attention has been paid to this dispute. Historians of philosophy have hardly taken notice of it. This is easy enough to understand: they primarily are concerned to understand the thought of philosophers. Moreover, the evidence for this debate is to be found almost exclusively in medical authors. And, finally, it is only recently that historians of philosophy have begun again to try seriously to understand the thought of the Hellenistic period, in particular, Hellenistic epistemology. It is precisely for this reason that one can hope that they soon will direct their efforts also to the epistemological debates within the schools of Hellenistic medicine. After all, there are obvious connections, which have been noticed a long time ago, between the philosophical debates and the debates within medicine. The Rationalists follow dogmatic philosophy, in particular the Stoics, whereas both Empiricists and Methodists rely on philosophical scepticism. Indeed, some of the later Empiricists, like Menodotus and Sextus Empiricus, are themselves major representatives of Pyrrhonean scepticism who can truly be considered philosophers. Thus it is obvious that the debate in medicine at that time is directly relevant to some of the main interests of current historians of ancient philosophy. Historians of medicine have naturally shied away from a discussion of the dispute, because philosophical debates are not their primary concern and because the technical nature of the debate makes it necessary to have some philosophical knowledge and, in particular, some knowledge of the history of Hellenistic philosophy to be able to follow the details of the dispute. Hence, it was classicists such as K. Deichgräber and L. Edelstein, who had taken a strong interest both in the history of ancient medicine and in the history of ancient philosophy, who began to open up the subject, though without being able to stimulate the further research which would have been necessary to get a complete and reasonably detailed and accurate picture of the debate as a whole, let alone to stimulate the wide interest in the subject it seems to deserve.

One reason for this, no doubt, is the relative inaccessibility of the evidence. Deichgräber collected a good deal of the evidence for the Empiricists in his admirable *Die griechische Empirikerschule*, but there is no corresponding collection for the Methodists, and it would be almost pointless to try to produce one for the Rationalists, given the enormous diversity of their positive views. But, though much of the evidence is scattered in obscure and often rare texts, four treatises tradition attributes to Galen are specifically devoted to the dispute. One of them, "On the

Best Sect", seems to be spurious, but three of them—"On the Sects for Beginners", "An Outline of Empiricism ", and "On Medical Experience'—are indeed Galenic. They constitute our main evidence for the dispute, jointly giving us enough detail to reconstruct the three competing views fairly accurately. But, since even these texts are not easily accessible, it seemed desirable to present them together in an English version. "An Outline of Empiricism", except for a short fragment in Greek, is extant only in a medieval Latin translation by Nicolaus of Reggio which, primarily because of its technique of translation, is rather difficult to read. It was edited by M. Bonnet and then reedited by Deichgräber in his *Die griechische Empirikerschule*. Apart from two fragments, "On Medical Experience" is extant only in an Arabic version, edited and translated into English by R. Walzer in a book which, because of the circumstances of its publication, is extremely rare. It is only "On the Sects for Beginners" which is easily available in an edition of the Greek text by G. Helmreich and an incomplete translation by A.J. Brock (*Greek Medicine*, London: 1929, pp. 130–51).

With the kind permission of the Wellcome Foundation and Oxford University Press, I have reproduced Walzer's translation of "On Medical Experience". Walzer did not translate from the Arabic the two sections of the text which are extant in Greek but instead printed the Greek text. Therefore, in those places, I have translated from the Greek rather than from the Arabic. Moreover, I have taken the liberty to transliterate the Greek words and, in one place, the Arabic which Walzer used in his English translation. It would have been more convenient to replace them by English translations, but I hesitated to tamper with Walzer's translation any further. The translations of "On the Sects for Beginners" and "An Outline of Empiricism" are mine. In one place, which is marked, I have decided to change the transmitted text, but in general I have tried to render the text as edited, even when I have had doubts about its correctness.

Galen

Though Galen's treatises present themselves as fair, balanced accounts of the respective positions of the three sects or schools of medicine and of the views they took of each other, they nevertheless do reflect a point of view, even a bias, on the matters at issue. Hence it might be best to begin with some introductory remarks on Galen and then to proceed to a brief discussion of the dispute which forms the subject matter of the three treatises.

First, a few remarks on Galen's life. We are unusually well informed about his life in general and about his literary activity, because Galen, throughout his voluminous writings, repeatedly refers to episodes in his life and to other writings of his. Claudius Galenus was born around A.D. 129 in Pergamum, a lively, wealthy city in Asia Minor, famous for its temple of Asclepius, a god of healing to whom Galen felt particularly devoted, but also famous as a center of learning, with a library which competed with that of Alexandria. His father, Nicon, was a well-educated architect, who provided his son not only with an inheritance which allowed Galen to live comfortably, securely, and independently but also with an education of encyclopedic range, with emphasis on the mathematical sciences, philosophy, and medicine. One gets the impression that Galen's upbringing was very conservative. On the one hand, it fostered a respect for tradition and its values; on the other, it encouraged independence within this traditional framework. Thus it was Galen's father who insisted that Galen should study philosophy with the exponents of all four schools of philosophy which were represented in his hometown, the Platonists (by a pupil of Gaius), the Peripatetics, the Stoics, and the Epicureans. To learn what there is to learn from all sides and to make up one's own mind is a recurrent theme in Galen's life. At the age of sixteen, he formally began to study medicine, both with Rationalists and with an Empiricist. When his father died, he left Pergamum to seek out the best teachers of medicine. He first went to Smyrna, where he also heard the Platonist Albinus, then to Corinth, then to Alexandria, where he stayed for roughly five years (A.D. 152–157). In 157 he returned to Pergamum to practice medicine. He soon was appointed doctor of the gladiators, a sad opportunity. But in 162 social unrest broke out in Pergamum. Galen left and slowly made his way to Rome, where he set out to make a reputation but also managed to make enemies. In 166 he left the city under obscure circumstances, only to be recalled from Pergamum in 168 by the emperors Marcus Aurelius and Lucius Verus, who wished him to join them with their army in their winter camp in Aquileia. But the plague broke out, and the court hurriedly moved to Rome. Galen would have liked to return to Pergamum, but he was named physician to Marcus Aurelius's son, Commodus, and later to Marcus Aurelius himself. Except for some travels, Galen stayed in Rome even after Marcus Aurelius's death, in spite of all the political turmoil which surrounded him. In 191, when the Temple of Peace burnt down, a large part of his library, in particular most of his philosophical writings, which he had deposited in the library of the temple, were lost. But Galen had found his place in Roman society, and there he stayed till his death around A.D. 200.

Galen was a prolific writer. Just those of his writings which are extant in Greek fill some twenty volumes. In addition, a good number of Galenic treatises are extant only in Arabic, such as "On Medical Experience" in this collection. Furthermore, there are treatises, such as the "Outline of Empiricism", which are only extant in Medieval Latin versions. But we know from Galen's extant works that what has come down to us is only a part of what he wrote. Not only does Galen constantly refer to writings now lost, there are also two extant monographs on his own works: "On My Own Writings" and "On the Order of My Writings". From all this, it is clear that Galen's literary activity covered mainly three areas: medicine, philosophy, and philology. But tradition has been very partial to his own medical writings, the majority of which are preserved, whereas his philosophical writings for the most part have been lost, and his philological writings have disappeared altogether. This is easily understood if one keeps in mind how selective tradition is. The corpus of Galen's medical writings presents itself as the sum of ancient medical knowledge, judiciously sifted, critically understood, and systematically organized by one who had carefully studied the whole tradition of Greek medicine from Hippocrates onwards and who had mastered the subject in all, or almost all, of its aspects so as to be able to judge and assimilate the contributions his predecessors had made to medicine. This was certainly the way Galen was received. With a few—though important—exceptions, such as Soranus's *Gynecology* and Dioscurides' *Materia Medica*, Galen just replaced the whole of the earlier medical literature. The greatest exception, of course, was Hippocrates himself, who, in no small part because of Galen's veneration for him, remained the classical medical author. But, though Galen also had a reputation as a philosopher, even in his lifetime, there was nothing clearly singular about his philosophical treatises, let alone about his philological writings, which would have protected them.

Galen, then, is known to us primarily as a physician, in antiquity second in fame only to Hippocrates, the father of the art of medicine, and also as the author of a vast corpus of medical writings which dominated medical thought into modern times, when his influence came to be felt as a burden and a yoke, much as, somewhat earlier, Aristotle's influence in philosophy and, in particular, in natural philosophy had come to be felt as stifling. Like Aristotelianism, Galenism had finally shown its severe limitations, but, since both had taken firm roots over the course of many centuries, it took a certain amount of violence to extirpate them. Thus Galen and Aristotle came to be seen in a negative, critical way, even if the criticism often was unfair and unbalanced. This continued for a long time, even though scholars no longer found it necessary or profitable to study their writings and hence had to rely for their critical judgments on received opinion. It was the classicists who, with a changed conception of their own subject, could turn again without prejudice and with a good amount of enthusiasm to this vast body of writings which sheds so much light on so many aspects of ancient life and, in particular, on medicine in antiquity, its theories and practice, the doctor's ethos and his position in society, and his attitude towards his clients. Thus we can also now see again Galen's positive contributions to the development of the medical art. We can appreciate as strengths some of the very features of Galen's work to which it owed its negative influence. It was his mastery of the medical tradition which made it seem largely unnecessary to continue to read earlier medical authors. It was his overpowering command of this vast subject which proved so discouraging to his successors. One cannot but admire the great care, the enormous skill, and the often considerable ingenuity with which Galen tried to discover the most minute details of anatomy and physiology by patient, careful observation. One may also sympathize with Galen's efforts to provide some theoretical framework for the discoveries he and his predecessors had made. But the framework he actually provides is rather schematic and dogmatic. It is supposed to define a position which does justice to as much of the tradition as possible. In spite of all his criticisms of his predecessors, there is a strong conservative and harmonizing element in Galen's thought which tends to make differences in point of view and conflicts appear much smaller than they actually were and which emphasizes areas of possible agreement, when real progress is made only by sharpening the differences and the conflicts, to bring them to a resolution on a higher level of understanding. Given his enormous learning and erudition, not just in medicine but also in the medical tradition, in physical theory, in logic, and, as we might say, in the philosophy of science and given the rapid decay which we observe in the succeeding centuries in almost all fields of learning, but certainly in logic, in physics, and in medical theory, Galen must have seemed to have achieved a resolution of these differences at a higher, philosophically grounded level of understanding. In fact, he had constructed just another theory which was loose and schematic enough to accommodate much of the medical tradition.

But, though Galen traditionally has been known as a medical authority, there also is, as we have already indicated, Galen the philosopher. Though most of his philosophical writings have been lost, even what remains is still quite impressive, at least in sheer size. There is an introduction to logic, the "Institutio Logica", the sad remnant of a considerable body of writings on logic. In particular, we have to deplore the loss of a large work "On Proof", of which only fragments remain (ed. I. v. Müller, *Abh. Bay. Akad. d. W.*, vol. 20, 1897). We have two treatises on causality ("De causis procatarcticis", ed. K. Bardong, 1937; "De causis contentivis", *CMG Suppl. Orient.* II, ed. M.C. Lyons et al., 1969); various treatises on moral psychology, in particular the "On the Passions of the Soul" (*CMG* V, 4, 1, 1, ed. W. DeBoer 1937); at least substantial fragments of a commentary on Plato's *Timaeus*, the voluminous "On the Views of Hippocrates and Plato" (*CMG* V, 4, 1, 2, ed. P. De Lacy, 1978–80), which among other things also deals with philosophical psychology; and, last but not least, the three treatises in the present collection on the nature of the art of medicine.

Galen was a philosopher of considerable reputation already in his lifetime. Though this reputation no doubt was due in good part to his authority as a medical writer, it would be rash to say that it was based entirely on his reputation as a physician. After all, Galen's philosophy has not been studied systematically as a whole, even though, as we have seen, various of his philosophical treatises are still extant and the rest of his writings abound in philosophical remarks, to which we have to add references in later authors to philosophical views he formulated in treatises now lost. The task of forming a critical view of Galen as a philosopher is made no easier by the fact that we have no coherent, reasonably comprehensive picture of the history of philosophy in the first two centuries of our era, and it is only against this background that we could judge to what extent there is any originality in Galen's philosophical thought. Galen had a respectable training in philosophy. He attended the lectures of four philosophers in Pergamum; he continued to study philosophy with Albinus in Smyrna; and, as late as his first stay in Rome, he seems to have attended the lectures of his friend, the Peripatetic Eudemus. He obviously was very widely read in philosophy, and there is no reason to think that his reading was superficial or perfunctory. Rather the opposite: as we know, e.g., from his two monographs on his own writings, he composed monographs and commentaries on a good number of the texts he had studied and on specific problems and questions these texts raised. He was obviously determined—and sufficiently confident in his own philosophical judgment—to make up his own mind in philosophy, too.

Though, as we will see, it is somewhat artificial to do so, we may distinguish three reasons for Galen's active interest in philosophy. Firstly, in Galen's time, it was part of the ideal of a reasonably educated person to have an interest in philosophy. His father certainly thought so, when he sent Galen to listen to the four major philosophers in Pergamum. But Galen's own interest clearly went beyond that. He clearly thought it mattered that one have one's own philosophical views. Secondly, he also believed that the perfect doctor has to be a philosopher. He devoted a whole treatise to this question ("That the Best Doctor Also Is a Philosopher", *Scripta Minora*, vol. II, ed. I. v. Müller, 1891). To understand this, one has to keep in mind that Galen thinks that the perfect doctor is scientifically trained and has mastered enough of the natural sciences to understand human physiology, anatomy, pathology, and pharmacology. Thus he has to know what in antiquity was called "physics" and was regarded as one of the three major parts of philosophy. Galen also took the view that, to be able to do science or even to understand it, one had to be thoroughly versed in logic; one had to know how to give proper definitions, make the right kinds of conceptual distinctions, give strict scientific proofs, be able logically to analyze proofs, and not fall victim to fallacies. So the Galenic physician also has to know logic. As to the third part of philosophy, ethics, it is easy even for us to see that being a good doctor requires the proper moral attitude and sound moral judgment. Ancient doctors had a lot to say about medical ethics, and it would be of interest to study this material systematically. Galen, in any case, thought that medicine presupposed all parts of philosophy, and his medical writings show abundantly how serious he was about this. Thirdly and finally, we have to keep in mind that it had been a long tradition in medicine, going back to the fifth century B.C., to take an interest in certain philosophical questions, e.g., the question of the nature of medical knowledge, explanation in medicine (hence an interest in causality), and the relation between body and soul. So it was only natural that Galen would join his great predecessors in medicine, who again and again had shown a more than passing interest in such questions.

How can one best characterize Galen's philosophical position in general terms? He himself claims that he does not want to subscribe to the position of any of the schools of philosophy. Hence it is fair to characterize him in his own words as an "eclectic" (cf. De libr. prop. I, *SM* II, p. 95; De dign. aft. 8, *CMG* V, 4, 1, 1, p. 28f.). But for us this term has the negative connotation of describing someone who does not have the philosophical power to construct his own system or to develop his own views, who rather somewhat uncritically borrows his thoughts from diverse sources. For obvious reasons, however, this is not how Galen looks at his own position, and it may indeed be unfair to see him this way. It seems, as we have seen, that his father had tried to foster a sense of independent judgment in him, when he sent him to attend the lectures of all four schools of philosophy. It is also noteworthy that Galen seems as a student to have taken issue with some of the views of his teachers, though he also had great admiration for some of them. Galen repeatedly criticizes in his works the dogmatic attitude of those who, in the face of truth, try to uphold the view of their school and who are slaves to received doctrine, whether this be in medicine or in philosophy. Thus Galen himself at least saw his eclecticism as a result of critical judgment, attachment to the truth, and moral strength. We may have a more modest view of his eclecticism, but we should grant that Galen made an effort to develop his own philosophical beliefs, that he quite sensibly thought reasonable beliefs were not the sole property of any one philosophical school, and that he believed it best to come to one's own views on the basis of a full understanding of the debates between the schools. That Galen did not have the philosophical power to bring about such a synthesis of the philosophical tradition in a meaningful and constructive fashion is another matter.

Though this is a subject of controversy, Galen's basic outlook, in spite of his professed eclecticism, nevertheless seems to be rather like that of a Platonist. He had studied in Pergamum with a student of Gaius, one of the most important Middle Platonic philosophers. When he went to Smyrna, he continued his philosophical studies with Albinus, another of the most influential Platonists of the period. He clearly has great admiration for Plato, who for him plays a role in philosophy somewhat similar to the role he attributes to Hippocrates in medicine. But Galen is by no means willing to accept Plato's views uncritically. Hence his eclecticism, at least on one level, is not the sign of an uncritical, dependent mind, but rather the opposite. On the other hand, one does have to acknowledge, in his case and even more so in that of his eclectic contemporaries, that it is an independence of mind within the limits of tradition, a somewhat backward-looking rather than a forward-looking independence, which tends to choose from among the old rather than to create the new.

It also has been argued that Galen basically is a Peripatetic. The reason for this is that Galen, in principle and in practice, attributes great importance to logic and to natural philosophy and in both relies quite heavily on Aristotle. But we have to remind ourselves that his logic is the syncretistic logic of his day which, in one form or another, we also find in Platonists such as Apuleius, Albinus, and the commentators on Aristotle, a logic which is very much influenced by Aristotle but still contains many elements of the logic of the Old Academy and is markedly influenced by Stoic logic. We also have to remember that, in logic and natural philosophy, the Platonic schools of late antiquity used the Aristotelian writings as textbooks. Hence we should not infer from the mere fact that Galen is heavily indebted to Aristotle in logic and physics that his basic outlook is Peripatetic. Though Galen rather resembles the Platonists of his day, there is one respect in which he differed quite markedly from them and from Plato himself, namely in his sceptical attitude towards what he regarded as speculation. Quite generally, Galen has a tendency to look at whole series of questions which had occupied philosophers for a long time and over which they had fallen into different camps, as questions one cannot settle, but only speculate about. Galen was determined not to waste his time on such speculations. Thus he thinks that there is no point in trying to take a stand on the questions of the nature of God, the substance of the soul, its embodiment and immortality, the eternity of the world, the number of worlds, or whether the world exists in a void (Plac. Hipp. et Plat. IX, 6, 19-9, 9, *CMG* V, 4, 1, 2, 1.576–600 ; In Hipp. de morb. ac. comm. I, 2, *CMG* V, 9, 1, p. 125; De subst. nat. fac. Kühn IV, 762 = De sent. 15.1; Quod animi mores 3, *SM* II, p. 36; De sent. 2 Nutton). It is not just that he thinks that one cannot have full confidence in one's views on such matters. He refuses to take *any* view on them. Since it is exactly on questions of this kind that the schools of philosophy are divided, Galen's attitude towards these questions goes some way to explain his refusal to identify himself with any of the schools.

This attitude no doubt is the result of the influence of scepticism. But, in spite of early temptations to the contrary, Galen was too impressed by the mathematical sciences to despair of the ability to reason towards theoretical truths. Hence he was also convinced that large areas of philosophy were immune to serious sceptical doubt, sufficiently so to be able to develop a logic, a physical theory (in the sense of a theory of nature in general), and a moral theory. For this he drew on Plato and the Platonists, on Aristotle and the Peripatetics, and even quite heavily on the Stoics. He does not hide his preference for Plato and Aristotle, and often enough he takes the Stoics to task for their innovations. In part this is due to his neoclassicist leanings, which are also reflected by his concern for proper Greek usage and by his philological interests. In this he just follows a general trend to revert to the models set by classical antiquity, a trend which begins in the second century B.C. and which in philosophy has the effect that Plato, Aristotle, and their immediate followers, such as Xenocrates and Theophrastus, come to be regarded as the "ancient" and "classical" philosophers, as opposed to the "younger" or "modern" philosophers of the Hellenistic age, in particular the Stoics and the Epicureans. But he also follows another tradition closely linked to the first one. This tradition underplays the differences between Plato and Aristotle, as if they had shared a basic common doctrine, and sees the Stoics largely as just putting this doctrine into new garb or, where this interpretation seems too far-fetched, as wilfully and arbitrarily breaking away from the tradition of the ancients. This way of looking at the matter allowed philosophers in this tradition to go to any lengths in assimilating into their own system the advances made by the Stoics, yet to continue to criticize them as entirely misguided. The only views one took to be distinctively Stoic were those one took exception to, while those views one found congenial were regarded as part of the common platonic heritage. In this way of looking at the history of philosophy, Galen does not differ from most of his contemporaries. If anything, it is easier for him than for them. That is, those questions which were thought to divide Plato and Aristotle and which were emphasized by the minority of later philosophers who rejected the harmonization of Plato and Aristotle were largely the very questions Galen regarded as speculative, e.g., the nature of God, the nature of the intellect, the nature of the human soul, the theory of ideas: what came to be regarded as the metaphysical questions.

It would be a mistake, though, to think of Galen as an agnostic in the modern sense. He readily accepts as fact that his father was inspired by a heaven-sent dream to have him study medicine, as if this was just another indication of the piety and rectitude of his father. He is not in the least critical of the assumption that there are divinely inspired dreams which prescribe a cure. As we can see from the "Outline of Empiricism" (chap. X, pp. 78–79 Deichgräber), he is even prepared to avail himself of therapeutic methods obtained in this way. In "On the Use of Parts" (III, 20), in which he tries to explain the functions of the different bodily parts, he calls his own treatise "a sacred book which I write as a hymn to our creator". It is easy to see how this fits into the long development in which theology as a philosophical discipline is more and more replaced by a theology of traditional belief or revelation, in which faith takes the place of reason, because human reason comes to be seen as limited, though the nature and the source of these limitations are as yet unclear.

On the other hand, if one looks for positive contributions Galen made to philosophy, the most promising place to search seems to be his discussions of the role reason and perception play in the acquisition of knowledge, in particular technical or scientific knowledge. This brings us to the debate which is the subject of our three treatises. Hence I will make some introductory remarks on this debate, before I return, in conclusion, to Galen, his position in the debate, and his contribution to the history of philosophy.

The Dispute on the Nature of Medical Knowledge

To understand the debate, one has to go back to the fifth century B.C., when the new art of medicine arose. Those who participated in the creation of this new art agreed that the traditional practice of medicine was insufficient, for reasons which in many ways are parallel to those for which the first philosophers thought that the traditional beliefs about the origin and the nature of the world were inadequate. They realized that there were many conflicting forms of traditional practices, that tradition itself provided no grounds to prefer one to another, and that some of those traditional practices involved beliefs an enlightened person could hardly accept, e.g., the belief that certain illnesses are due to possession by a demon. Moreover, they realized that traditional practice was not particularly successful and often could even see why it was bound to be damaging. The corpus of Hippocratic writings is full of such criticisms of traditional medicine, showing into what disrepute medicine and its practitioners had fallen in the fifth century, at least among the educated. But, though it was clear to some that traditional practice had to be critically reevaluated and replaced by a medical practice which would stand up to criticism, it was by no means obvious how one was to arrive at a new art of medicine. The philosophers provided a clear suggestion as to what was to be done. They had been trying to give a generally acceptable account of the world and its most interesting features. As their theories grew more powerful, they naturally tried to see to what extent they could also use those theories to explain the constitution of human beings, the way they function, and even the way they fail to function properly, especially in the fifth century, when the attention of philosophers quite generally turned to human beings. From this time onwards, at least into Hellenistic times, the philosophers regarded human physiology and pathology as part of natural philosophy. Aristotle claimed (De sensu 436^a 17–22) that it was the task of the natural philosopher to discuss the principles of health and disease, and he stated that this was indeed what most natural philosophers did (ibid. and De resp. 480^b 28–30). If we look at the evidence, this testimony seems to be borne out. Pythagoras, Alcmaeon, Empedocles, Anaxagoras, Diogenes of Apollonia, Democritus, and others had more or less detailed medical views or even wrote medical treatises (for Democritus, e.g., cf. D.L. ix, 46). Plato's *Timaeus*, with its long discussion of the constitution of the human body and of health and disease and its causes, gives us a clear idea of how natural it was for philosophers to engage in medical theory.

Thus the doctors who tried to develop a new art of medicine quite understandably tended to assume that the way to accomplish this task was to develop a medical theory which would allow one to understand the nature of the various diseases, to determine their causes, and, on this basis, to find the appropriate remedies. Such a theory would finally allow one critically to evaluate traditional medical practices.

This view was generally adopted, though it met with some opposition. The author of "On Ancient Medicine" claimed that there was a simple way in which mankind actually had made enormous progress in medicine over the ages. Men had learned from dire experience, by trial and error, what was conducive and what was detrimental to health. Not only did he claim that one should not abandon this simple method in favor of fanciful philosophical theories, which do not lead anywhere, he also argued that good doctors in practice relied on this experience anyway, since their theories were too vague and too general to guide their practice.

The majority of doctors, though, thought that they needed some theory which would guide and explain their practice. What they disagreed about was what kind of theory they should adopt, not just in the sense that they disagreed about the truth or falsehood of the various theoretical claims, but about the very nature of the theory, though it took some time for the issues involved to become clear. One choice the doctors faced was whether they should just adopt a philosophical theory of nature in general and of the constitution of human beings in particular, or whether they should try to work out their own theory. Some doctors obviously had grave misgivings about just adopting a philosophical theory. The author of the Hippocratic treatise "Nature of Man", for example, though he readily acknowledged the need for some kind of account of human physiology, was equally firm in his view that in medicine there was no use for the kinds of accounts in terms of the ultimate principles of physics which the philosophers liked to give. The doctors were looking for a theory which would suit their specific needs and which fitted their experience and observation. Given their knowledge of the human body, they naturally thought that a proper theory of physiology should take due account of and explain the features which they had come to think of as particularly relevant. In this respect, not only must the philosophical theories have seemed too global and too schematic to them, but they must have wondered how a philosophical theory, given the way it was arrived at, namely by rather global considerations, without particular attention to, let alone specialized knowledge of, the human body, could ever be sufficient. From this point onwards, there was a strong tendency among doctors to think that they had a right to develop their own physical theory and to have their own views about how such a theory was to be formed. It was in this way that a tradition of independent philosophical thought arose in medicine. It is as part of this tradition that we must view the later debate.

The fourth and the beginning of the third century B.C. saw enormous advances in medical theory. In particular, one has to mention the work of Diocles, of Praxagoras, of Herophilus, and of Erasistratus. One can notice, especially in Diocles and in Herophilus, a certain uneasiness about the status of medical theory and about its relation to the physical theory of the philosophers and to observation. Diocles warned against the tendency to look for a theoretical causal account for everything (*Galen*, Kühn VI, p. 455). He explained that such knowledge rarely is of practical use. He also maintained that we should treat many facts of nature as primitive, rather than try to explain them in terms of some questionable theory which would serve no further purpose. Herophilus, too, took the view that in medicine one often has to take as a given or a principle what in the true nature of things, if we could only ascertain it, would turn out to be a derivative truth (cf. Anonymus Lond. XXI, 21; Galen De meth. med., Kühn X, p. 107). In Herophilus we already find doubts about the way medical theory appeals to causes (cf. Galen De causis procatarcticis 197 ff.). But, in spite of this uneasiness, there is the general conviction that, underlying the phenomena of health and illness, there is a reality which we can grasp by means of reason, by making the right inferences from what we observe and by relying on some general theory which is supposed somehow to capture this reality, and that it is in terms of this theory that we have to understand and practically deal with the phenomena of health and illness.

By the beginning of the third century B.C., though, there had been a proliferation of such theories. Each school tried to defend a particular theory against its rivals and thus came to have a vested interest in maintaining this view. There were not just students of Herophilus and Erasistratus, there arose sects of Herophileans and Erasistrateans. Towards the middle of the third century, this state of affairs provoked a strong reaction, which gave rise to Empiricism, the view that the actual knowledge a competent doctor relies on in treating his patients is entirely a matter of experience, and that hence there is no need for medical theories, with their postulation of theoretical entities to be inferred or grasped by reason, such entities as atoms, invisible pores, the void, essences, forces, and hidden causes. The Empiricists attacked all existing schools as putting undue trust in the power of reason and labeled them "Rationalist". Though a lot divided the schools attacked as Rationalist, they all felt united in their defense of reason and joined in the counterattack on the

Empiricists, arguing that mere experience would never account for an art of medicine, the kind of expertise one could expect from an accomplished doctor. The question, as it is put by Galen in the first chapter of "On the Sects for Beginners", then, is whether experience alone suffices to arrive at the art of medicine or whether reason, too, is necessary.

The question is somewhat curious, as one would imagine that the Empiricists would not want to proscribe the use of reason quite generally. It is difficult to see how there could be any satisfactory medical practice which does not involve some amount of reasoning, some deliberation. It is clear that the Empiricists did not want to deny this, but it is difficult to say precisely what they wanted to deny, when they rejected the use of reason. There seems to have been some unclarity and some wavering in their position on this question, which Galen reports on in Chapter 12 of the "Outline of Empiricism". What the Empiricists clearly wanted to reject were formal inferences, either deductive or inductive, in particular inferences by means of which people were supposed to get a grasp on the theoretical truths which underlie what they could observe, and most emphatically those inferences which were supposed to lead to theoretical truths concerning theoretical entities, like the atoms, which can only be grasped by reason. The kind of reasoning they were willing to allow was the kind of reasoning we use in everyday life, when we consider things, think about things, and when such thoughts suggest to us an answer to the question which made us think about the subject, because we did not have a ready answer. But this is not a matter of making formal inferences according to the canons of some logic; it is a matter of becoming sufficiently convinced of a view, having thought about the matter for long enough. The Empiricists called reasoning in this sense "epilogism", and they insisted that this kind of reasoning could never lead to theoretical truths about theoretical entities, but only to the kinds of truths discovered in ordinary life. In any case, the question whether experience alone might suffice to arrive at the art of medicine or whether reason, too, was needed, was understood by both sides in the debate to refer to a special use of reason by means of which, according to the Rationalists, theories are arrived at.

This debate within medicine also has to be seen against the background of another, much more general debate, about which we unfortunately know very little today. It seems that, at the end of the fifth and in the course of the fourth century, some authors had taken the view that certain important bodies of technical knowledge or expertise were mere matters of experience and that perhaps all knowledge was of this kind. Plato in the *Gorgias* makes Socrates criticize Polus' claim that rhetoric is the highest of all human arts, the master discipline, by arguing that rhetoric, at least as Gorgias and Polus conceive of it, is merely a matter of experience and knack or practice [tribe] and not an art [techne]. But there is good reason to believe that Polus himself did in fact hold the view that rhetorical knowledge is a matter of experience (Ar. Met 981ª 4), and it is certainly no accident that two terms Plato here uses to discredit Gorgianic rhetoric, namely empeiria 'experience' and tribe 'knack' or 'practice', are both terms later Empiricists used in a positive sense.

There also was the view that political knowledge was just a matter of experience (Philodemus Rhet. B, I, 27–28). Some may even have held the view that medical knowledge is just a matter of experience. For this, in a way, is the expressed opinion of the author of "On Ancient Medicine". Moreover, some later Empiricists believed they had found the origins of Empiricism in Acron of Akragas, a fifth-century follower of Empedocles (Galen, "Outline of Empiricism", I, p. 42, 21 D.; Ps. Galen Isagoge, vol. XIV, p. 683 Kühn). Finally, Erasistratus and possibly Herophilus found it worthwhile to argue against the suggestion that medicine is a matter of experience (Galen, "De sect. ingred." 5 SM III, p. 9, 15; De meth. med. Kühn, X, p. 184; Pliny, Historia naturalis, 29, 5, 6). These arguments almost certainly predate the rise of Empiricism and hence most likely address themselves to an earlier suggestion that knowledge of medicine can be based on experience alone.

In any case, Plato and Aristotle quite firmly reject the idea that an art or a science can be a matter of mere experience. A true art or science has to be based on truly general knowledge, which only reason and not experience can provide us with. However much our experience may suggest that something is quite generally true, experience itself does not justify this assumption. Only reason can. Experience does not give us any explanations but, at best, facts. But we do expect from an expert or from a scientist that he can explain why he thinks what he thinks and why he does what he does. Experience does not allow us to deal with new or unforeseen cases, unless they are like those we have encountered in experience. Reason can deal with new cases by analyzing them and subsuming them under the various general truths which are applicable to them. In this view that experience does not suffice for an art or a science, the physicians followed the philosophers. Obviously the conception we find, at least in the rhetorical tradition in the fourth century, that an art or a science is just a matter of experience, was not sufficiently worked out to withstand the strong and determined attack the philosophers made against it.

There was another relevant fact. We can see from Plato's Laws (cf. 720 A–C; 857 C–D) that there were two kinds of doctors in the fourth century. There were the physicians who had acquired an understanding of the workings of nature in general and of the human body in particular and who tried to practice medicine in the light of their theoretical understanding. There were also men who might, for example, have worked as assistants to a physician, who had learned enough from experience to take care of a good variety of medical problems, without having any theoretical understanding of their practice. It is clear from Plato's description that this distinction was associated with a social distinction, that between free doctors, who treated free men, and slave doctors or doctors of very inferior status, who treated slaves. Thus, when the physicians emphasized the importance of a theoretical understanding as the basis for medical practice, they were also emphasizing their education and their social status and thus distancing themselves from the lowly practitioners of a modest craft.

For this reason, when the Empiricists argued that even the expertise of the most competent and learned doctor is nothing but a matter of experience, they not only had to develop a more detailed account of experience than their predecessors in the rhetorical tradition had done, they also had to show that experience itself could generate a competence which would distinguish the learned doctor from the lowly practitioner.

To achieve this, they followed a twofold line of argument. On the one hand, they tried to explain positively how mere experience might suffice to give rise to as complex an expertise as that of a competent doctor. On the other hand, relying on Sceptical arguments, they tried to undermine any confidence in medical theory. They argued that the theoretical assumptions which characterized these theories involved the postulation of unobservable theoretical entities, such as atoms or invisible pores, whose existence was questionable and that these assumptions were sheer unverifiable speculation. The competing theories had proliferated because the doctors had given themselves to such speculation, and because they were a matter of mere speculation, there was no way in which one could adjudicate between them. Whereas in a proper art or science we should expect that the experts can come to an agreement as to what is true and what is false, medical theorizing seems to lead to ever greater disagreement. If we do assume that, as early as the fourth or even the end of the fifth century, there already was the notion that medicine should be based entirely on experience, then the distinctive features of the Empirical school are the detail with which it tries to substantiate this view and in particular its alliance with scepticism that allows it to support its view by an attack on any form of Rationalism.

There is reason to suppose that the Empiricist position evolved considerably over time. We know from Galen's "Outline of Empiricism" that different Empiricists provided different formulations of their view, and

Galen himself thought that there were substantial disagreements among Empiricists. This must be correct, since Sextus Empiricus, who was without a doubt an Empiricist himself, to the great puzzlement of the commentators, in the "Outlines of Pyrrhonism" (I, 236 ff.) criticizes Empiricism and claims to find Methodism in some ways more acceptable. The explanation almost certainly is that, as Pyrrhonean Scepticism evolved after Aenesidemus in the first century B.C., Empiricism, to the extent that it relied on Pyrrhonean Scepticism, had to become more sophisticated. To Galen and to Sextus Empiricus, at least some of the major Empiricists, e.g., Menodotus, seemed to be rather dogmatic, not only in their rejection of theoretical truths concerning hidden entities, but perhaps also in their reliance on perception. The more sophisticated version of Empiricism, which we can gather from Galen's "Outline" and extrapolate from Sextus Empiricus, is not a position according to which, for dogmatic reasons, perception is given a privileged status and experience is taken to be just the accumulated observation of what has been perceived. It is rather the life experience which suggests, among other things, that the way to acquire medical expertise is to observe. The Empiricist position itself is supposed to be a matter of experience and not itself something arrived at by a priori reasoning. So we do have good reason to assume that the Empiricist position developed, but at present we know next to nothing about this development. The first Empiricists, Philinus of Cos (ca. 250 B.C.), Serapio of Alexandria (ca. 225 B.C.), and Glaucias of Tarent (ca. 175 B.C.), are little more than names to us, as far as their Empiricism is concerned, and the views Galen reports on are largely the views of such later Empiricists as Menodotus and Theodas of Laodicea, in the first part of the second century A.D.

The view of the Empiricists seems to amount to something like the following: The bases of medical expertise or of any expertise are one's own observations [autopsia]. But obviously expertise is not acquired in the ordinary course of events; otherwise, everybody would be an expert. We have to explain how it comes about that the medical expert has a special expertise which distinguishes him not only from the layman, who after all has some experience with medical matters, but also from the lowly practitioner, who has a fair amount of experience, though of a limited kind. Moreover, we have to take notice of the fact that one's own observations are always quite limited and will not suffice to deal with all cases one may be expected to deal with. We can solve both of these problems by doing two things: (i) We carefully study the reports other doctors give of their experience, what they tried in which cases with what success [historia]. This is a procedure ordinary life experience suggests; we often rely on the reports of others, when our own experience of a matter is insufficient. (ii) Ordinary life experience also suggests that, in cases in which we do not have any experience or in which we do not have ready the remedies our experience suggests, we proceed by transition to the similar, i.e., that we use remedies similar to the ones we normally use or that we use the remedies which we normally use in similar cases. Now, the successful use of both history and the transition to the similar requires a lot of experience which is described and discussed in detail. We have to find out that not all authors are equally trustworthy; we have to learn to weigh the evidence they supply. We have to learn what is to count as "similar". But in the end, we will come to have a rich experience of our own, based on our own observations, on our ability to make optimal use of history, and on our facility to make the right transitions to the similar. By means of the last, we will increase medical knowledge, once our transition has proved to be successful and has been tested over and over again. Hence it is this ability, together with the historical learning, which distinguishes the great doctor from both the layman and the simple practitioner.

Now, nowhere in all this does one have to refer to any theoretical, unobservable entities; rather, one just observes particulars, the effects certain conditions, circumstances, events have on them, and the effects the remedies one uses have on them. If one has enough experience, one will be able to say whether something precedes, accompanies, or follows something else invariably, for the most part, as it may happen, or rarely. Statements to this effect will form the theorems which one draws on in one's practice. But it is important to realize that the way one draws on these theorems is not the way the Rationalist claims one ought to draw on theorems. It is not that one takes these theorems to be theoretical truths, subsumes a particular case under them, and draws the appropriate logical inference for the particular case. It is rather that, in virtue of one's general knowledge and of one's knowledge of these theorems, a particular case will suggest a particular thought or a particular course of action with varying intensity, and one correspondingly follows or does not follow the suggestion. Or, rather, the particular case will suggest a particular thought or a particular course of action in such a way that, depending on our experience, we have higher or lower expectations as to the trustworthiness of the thought and the appropriateness of the action. Thus, if one knows from experience that a certain remedy helps in a certain kind of case, this means that, if one encounters a case of this kind, it will strongly suggest to one to apply the remedy that invariably has helped. If, on the other hand, the remedy has helped only occasionally, our expectations as to its success in this case will be correspondingly lower. So what expertise does is provide the doctor with an abundance of suggestions of different force, the strongest of which, with increasing experience, will tend to be more and more reliable, for, if the treatment fails, this failure will diminish the force of the suggestion or the degree of confidence we have in it. Therefore, neither the way we acquire this general knowledge nor the way we actually use it in practice involves the use of formal inferences, let alone inferences to and from theoretical truths about theoretical entities. It is this kind of view which the Empiricists work out in great detail, to show that a doctor has no need for Rationalist reasoning and the kind of theory it gives rise to.

Thus the Empiricist can go on to argue against each and any Rationalist medical theory, using the kind of sceptical arguments with which we are familiar from Sextus Empiricus: that we have no reason to accept these theories, that they are ill-founded. But he can also agree that, even if there were a way to justify them, there would be no need for such theories, for what we need in any case is experience, and experience, as we have seen, suffices.

Just as the Empiricists rely on Sceptical arguments for their attack on the Rationalists, the Rationalists seem to rely heavily on the philosophers for their own positive views concerning the nature of medical knowledge, and, depending on their philosophical leanings, they tend to adopt rather different epistemological views. There is no one general positive view all Rationalists share. All they agree on is that experience is not sufficient to explain an art or science and that we have to appeal to the cognitive powers of reason which provide us with knowledge beyond what is given to us by experience. In particular, they allow us to make inferences and assumptions about entities which can never be observed but which are accessible only to reason. There are many different ways in which reason may be supposed to have such cognitive powers. Followers of Plato and Aristotle appealed to the powers of the intellect to grasp immediate, ultimate truths. Stoics and Epicureans, each in their own way, believed in innate ideas, conceptions which naturally arise in us and which we draw on in our reasoning. Platonists, Peripatetics, and Stoics believed in intrinsic relations between truths which reason can grasp and which allow reason to make inferences according to the rules of logic. But it is noteworthy that, as likely as not, when we actually learn something about the epistemological views of a Rationalist doctor, it turns out that his view goes well beyond what we are already familiar with from the history of philosophy. Obviously, Diocles' view, as reflected by the long fragment in Galen's *Hygieina* (Kühn VI, p. 455 H), is not just a reflection of Aristotle's views. Herophilus' views, especially his remarks on causes, a topic of central importance to a Rationalist, seem to be tinged by scepticism, as if our medical theories were never a matter of knowledge but only of reasonable belief. Asclepiades of Bithynia is conventionally thought of as an Epicurean, but neither his atomism nor his epistemology is straightforwardly Epicurean. A lot more work needs to be done on rather meager sources to get a more comprehensive idea of the various positive views of the Rationalists.

As to their criticisms of Empiricism, we are reasonably well informed, especially when it comes to Asclepiades of Bithynia, since Galen, in his "On the Sects for Beginners" and in particular in his "On Medical Experience", spells out in some detail what Asclepiades' objections were.

Asclepiades is a pivotal figure in this debate in two respects. First, the dispute between Rationalists and Empiricists flares up again due to his violent attacks on Empiricism, which will provoke an equally violent response, e.g., on the part of Menodotus. Second, we can also trace the origins of Methodism back to him, not to his epistemological but to his physiological views. Asclepiades' medical position is characterized by the assumption that internal diseases are due not to the humours but in general to the disruption of the orderly flow of the atoms through the channels or pores which permeate the relatively fixed concatenation of atoms constituting the frame of the body. In particular, he assumed that many diseases were caused by the disruption of the flow of atoms through minute invisible pores whose existence had to be inferred by reason.

Now, there is a controversy about the precise origin of Methodism which I do not want to enter into here, because its discussion would invoke complex questions of chronology, for instance. But it seems that the Methodist position was arrived at in two steps: (i) Asclepiades' view of at least certain diseases was generalized to the view that all diseases are a matter of undue constriction of pores, of undue dilation of pores, or of the combination of the two. (ii) Whereas, in Asclepiades' theory, these states of constriction, dilation, or a combination of both were hidden states, to be inferred from the symptoms, the Methodists assumed that they were phenomenal states, that one could train oneself to see that this example is a case of dilation, this is a case of constriction, and this a case of both. The first step was taken by Themison and his followers in the second part of the first century B.C.; the second step was taken by Thessalus in the first part of the first century A.D., if not earlier. Since Thessalus was the great propagandist of "the method", as it was called, he came to be thought of as the founder of the school, though one also realized that the movement somehow went back to Themison and ultimately had its roots in Asclepiades' position. To understand why the Methodists took the second step, which gave their view the distinctive character that radically distinguished it from Asclepiades' view, we have to consider how the Methodists could find a position besides Empiricism and Rationalism, when the two seemed to exhaust all possible options.

When the Methodists claimed that all diseases are, as they put it, manifest communities or generalities, i.e., a manifest state of constriction, or dilation, or the combination of both, they meant to agree with the Empiricists that the diseases are not hidden states, to be inferred by reason from observable symptoms, but manifest states, open to observation. They agreed with the Empiricists quite generally that the beliefs the doctor bases his practice on should not involve reference to hidden, theoretical entities, like Asclepiades' atoms and invisible pores, since we do not have certain knowledge of those entities and should not base our practice in matters of health and illness, let alone of life and death, on anything but certain knowledge. But exactly for this reason, experience does not suffice either, because all experience can give us is more or less reliable generalizations. Experience itself cannot provide us with the assurance that what has worked a hundred times will work on the one hundred and first time. In this respect, the Rationalists were right when they claimed that the doctor requires more than experience, namely, the firm knowledge that is to be obtained only by reason. It is reason and not experience which tells us that somebody who is constricted needs to be dilated and that somebody who is dilated needs to be constricted. It takes no experience to see that, just simple reason. Similarly it takes no experience, but simple reason, to see that a particular form of constriction or dilation needs the corresponding form of dilation or constriction. This is a matter of certain knowledge. It is only when we follow reason into speculations about the nature of things, causes, essences, forces, and other hidden entities that we leave the realm of certain knowledge and follow mere opinion. It was a mistake on the part of the Rationalists to think that certain knowledge could and in fact had to be gained in this way, and, moreover, it was a mistake to think that medical practice could be based on conclusions thus obtained.

To defend this view of Rationalist theories, the Methodists, just like the Empiricists, relied on Sceptical arguments. But, whereas the Empiricists utterly rejected all theory, often in a rather dogmatic fashion, the Methodists allowed theory, as long as it was understood that theory is mere speculation and that one's practice should not be based on it.

Methodism had a great success in Rome. Nevertheless, the aggressive way it was propounded by Thessalus could not but offend more traditionally minded doctors. When Hippocrates had said that life is short and art long, Thessalus claimed that life was long and art short, a matter of six months. This was a deliberate affront not only to all those who venerated Hippocrates but also to all those who, like Galen, prided themselves on their long and no doubt expensive medical training. It seems fairly clear that Methodism was also felt and presumably meant to be a social threat: a clear medical doctrine to be learned in six months, even by slaves and the poor, who had not the education to master the secrets of philosophy, mathematics, and the whole of learned medical tradition going all the way back to Hippocrates.

Galen certainly spoke of the Methodists with a good amount of bile. Little would one gather from his general discussion of the Methodists and of Thessalus and his followers that one of the greatest ancient doctors, Soranus, was a Methodist, for whose work, moreover, Galen himself had the greatest respect. But, since Galen is our main source for Methodism, our evidence makes it somewhat difficult to appreciate properly whatever subtleties Methodist thought may have involved.

Galen's Position in the Debate

As we have noted, Galen's reports of the dispute are somewhat coloured by his own position, especially when it comes to the Methodists. Here, too, Galen refuses to join any of the parties in the debate (De libr. prop. 1, SM II, 95), trying rather to take his own stand, from which he then judges the different positions.

It may have been Galen's influence which accounts in good part for the fact that, in the course of the third century, doctors seem to have lost their interest in this dispute. Galen certainly tries to give one the impression that he has found a position from which one can see that there is an important place in medicine for the Empiricist approach, just as there is a need for Rationalist theory, that the two do not exclude but rather complement and supplement each other, indeed, that they depend on each other in an accomplished doctor.

Galen sees no merit in the epistemological position of the Methodists. But he does have considerable sympathy for Empiricism, which goes back all the way to his days as a student in Pergamum, where one of his teachers was the Empiricist Aeschrion. This sympathy is apparent not just from the medical writings, but also from the two monographs he devoted to Empiricism and which are to be found in this collection: "On Medical Experience" and "An Outline of Empiricism". Though Galen, in particular in the latter treatise, does criticize certain Empiricists, both treatises on the whole are defenses of Empiricism against certain standard Rationalist criticisms. The Rationalists had claimed that experience does not suffice to arrive at the art of medicine, i.e., to gain the kind of expertise we expect in a competent, artful doctor. In the "Outline of Empiricism", Galen tells us that the very point of writing this monograph was to show that somebody could acquire the art of medicine by experience without the use of reason, though such a person would not be able to find out all that there is to be known about medicine (chap. 12, Deichgräber p. 88). But the qualification also indicates why Galen thinks that the Empiricist position is inadequate. There are matters of use to the doctor which are not known by experience, but by reason, in virtue of a medical theory of the Rationalist type (De methodo med. V, 1, Kühn X, p. 306; XIV, 5, Kühn X, 962; De comp. med. p. gen. VI, 7, Kühn XIII, 887), just as there is useful medical knowledge that is won only by experience (cf. ibid.). Thus the Empiricists are wrong when they claim that the whole of the art of medicine is a matter of experience. They are also wrong in rejecting the use of reason and the so-called rational method to arrive at a well-founded medical theory, for not only does human reason allow us to arrive at such theories, such theories also are necessary to understand and explain medical practice. Experience may provide us with facts, but it cannot provide us with their explanation (De simpl. med. II, 5, Kühn XI, p. 476; De caus. puls. III, 1, Kühn IX, p. 106). So it is true that Empiricist medicine, as opposed to what the Rationalists had claimed, truly is an art, a technical expertise, but it fails to be scientific. In this way, Galen can claim to be neither a Methodist nor an Empiricist nor a Rationalist.

He takes the matter a step further, and it is this further step which makes his position rather interesting, if not original. Galen does believe in the Rationalist idea of a science based on first principles, axioms which are not mere hypotheses to be confirmed by experience, but which are seen by reason to be true by virtue of some insight into the nature of things. But he also reveals a surprising amount of diffidence as to how we know that reason has grasped the right principles and arrived at the truth by derivation from these principles. Thus he says that he wishes everything were a matter of perception; for then there soon would be no more disagreement and no need to appeal to reason to settle doubts (De simpl. med. II, 2, Kühn XI, p. 462). He also tells us that experience is the most reliable criterion (De simpl. med. I, 40, Kühn XI, 456). If theory and observation disagree, it is the theory which has to be rejected (De fac. nat. I, 13, 501 III, p. 132; II, 8, 500 III, p. 186).

Thus Galen comes to suggest that we should, on the one hand, learn as much as possible from experience and develop a body of empirical knowledge that is quite uncontaminated by any theory, and, on the other, develop a Rationalist theory, then check the results of the theory against our body of empirical knowledge (De methodo medendi I, 4, Kühn X, p. 31; II, 7, Kühn X, p. 127; III, 1, Kühn X, p. 159; IV, 3, Kühn X, p. 246).

Whatever the merits of this suggestion may be, the fact still remains that Galen's position on this debate discouraged further discussion. It now was perfectly all right to try to acquire a body of empirical knowledge, as the Empiricists had done, as long as one did not go on to reject theory, and it was similarly perfectly all right to construct theories, as the Rationalists had done, as long as these theories did not conflict with experience and as long as one did not go on to deny that there could be a whole body of knowledge based on experience or even to deny that there could be anything known by experience. Put this way, Galen's position just seemed too sensible to be rejected, and it must have been difficult to see why there ever had been such excitement about the issue, particularly when, in the third century A.D., Scepticism lost all attraction. Without some sympathy for and understanding of Scepticism, it is difficult to understand and to appreciate the antitheoretical bias of Empiricism. Given Galen's own somewhat less than confident attitude as to the actual truth of any theory we may have, the difference between Rationalism and Methodism must have seemed less clear-cut, too. This is especially true if, in this case also, one no longer appreciated the Sceptical background of the position. Thus it may well be the case that Galen here, too, instead of carrying the issue a step further by, for example, critically reexamining the Rationalist notion of a science, rather changed the issue in a way which would allow him to propose a solution which seemed to accommodate the best the tradition had to offer, and this with so much learning and persuasiveness that it would have taken a lot to realize that the real problems which had given rise to the debate might have been put out of sight but had not disappeared.

But, though I think that Galen ultimately did not do justice to the issue that had provoked this debate, another element in Galen's thought on the matter did have an important future. Galen thought that the role of reason and observation in knowledge is twofold. Reason and observation are instrumental, in that they serve to arrive at the truth, but they also play a critical role, in that they are used to decide or to confirm the truth of a view which one already has arrived at. Galen made a great effort to spell out in detail how reason and observation are to be used in either case. Traditionally philosophers had concentrated on a rational method of proof. Aristotle's *Analytics*, in particular the *Posterior Analytics*, had served this purpose, and Stoic logic had focussed on the same aim. What one seemed to lack, though, was a rational method of discovery, an *ars inveniendi*. We see an interest in such a method in Cicero, not surprisingly, given the needs of an orator (Topica 6; De orat. II, 157–59; De fin. IV, 10). There is a tradition of such an interest which we also find in Quintilian and in Boethius (In Cic. top. 1045 A) and which expands enormously during the Renaissance. But Cicero's own remarks show that this is an interest which is already recognized by the philosophers of his time, if not by the Stoics, then at least by the Peripatetics. And, indeed, we do find reflections of this interest, e.g., in the account of Aristotle's philosophy in Diogenes Laertius (V, 28–29) and in Alexander of Aphrodisias' commentary on Aristotle's *Prior Analytics* (p. 1, 7 ff). In the syncretistic logic of late antiquity, beginning with Middle Platonists such as Albinus (cf. Isagoge 5, p. 156 Hermann), such a method of invention or discovery occurs under the name of *analysis* or *analytics*. Thus Galen can rely on some tradition when he tries to work out in detail the method of synthesis or composition and in particular the method of analysis or resolution. There is good reason to believe that his remarks on synthesis and analysis were directly and indirectly of great influence on scientific thought in the Renaissance. From the thirteenth century onwards, Galen's writings in Latin translation played an increasing role in the medical schools of the universities and had an influence far beyond the faculties of medicine, in particular in those universities, such as Padua, which were dominated by the medical school. Two treatises were studied with particular care, the *Ars medica* and the "On the Method of Healing," which also came to be known respectively as the *Ars parva* or the *Tegni* (i.e., *techne*) and the *Ars magna* or the *Megategni*. Now, the *Tegni* starts out with rather obscure remarks about analysis and synthesis, but it was also a text which was widely lectured and commented on. So it gave ample opportunity for reflection on the ways of scientific discovery and of scientific demonstration within the framework of a Galenic position. For this position, there was ample evidence in his other writings, but in particular in the *Megategni*, which in its introductory pages (De meth. med. I, 3, Kühn X, p. 29) makes the claim that there is a systematical, logical method of discovery and which in fact itself has as its aim to spell out the rational method of discovering the appropriate treatment for a given disease.

It is presumably here that we have to look for a positive, lasting contribution Galen made to philosophical thought.

Bibliography

1 The standard edition of Galen's collected works is C.G. Kühn, *Galeni Opera Omnia*, Leipzig: 1821–33 (repr. Hildesheim: 1965). This edition is slowly being replaced by critical editions in the *Corpus Medicorum Graecorum* (Leipzig: 1914 ff.). In particular, I would like to refer to *Galeni Pergameni Opera Minora*, ed. J. Marquardt, I. v. Müller, G. Helmreich, 3 vols., Leipzig: 1884–93.

2 The following editions served as the basis for this collection: "De sectis ingredientibus" [On the Sects for Beginners], ed. G. Helmreich, in *Galeni Pergameni Opera Minora*, vol. III, Leipzig: 1893; "Subfiguratio empirica" [An Outline of Empiricism], ed. K. Deichgräber, *Die griechische Empirikerschule*, Berlin: 1930 (repr. with additions Berlin: 1965); "On Medical Experience", ed. R. Walzer, Oxford: 1944.

3 On Galen in general, see G. Sarton, *Galen of Pergamon*, Lawrence, Kansas: 1965[3]; O. Temkin, *Galenism*, Ithaca: 1971; V. Nutton, ed., *Galen: Problems and Prospects*, London: 1981; L. Garcia Ballester, *Galeno*, Madrid: 1972; for lists of writings, editions, and questions of authenticity, see K. Schubring, "Bemerkungen zu der Galenausgabe von Karl Gottlieb Kühn und zu ihrem Nachdruck", in C.G. Kühn, *Galeni Opera Omnia*, repr. 1965, vol. I, pp. v–lxii.

4 On Galen's life and writings, see J. Walsh, "Galen's Writings and Influences Inspiring Them", *Ann. Med. Hist.* vol. 6, 1934, pp. 1–30, 142–49, vol. 7, 1935, pp. 428–37, 570–89, vol. 8, 1936, pp. 65–90, vol. 9, 1937, pp. 34–61; J. Ilberg, "Über die Schriftstellerei des Klaudios Galenos", *Rhein. Mus. f. Philol.* vol. 44, 1889, pp. 207–39, vol. 47, 1892, pp. 489–514, vol. 51, 1896, pp. 165–96, vol. 52, 1897, pp. 591–623; K. Bardong, "Beiträge zur Hippokrates- und Galenforschung", *Nachr. Akad. d. W. Göttingen, phil.-hist. Kl.*, vol. 7, 1942, 577–640.

5 On Galen's philosophy, see Ph. DeLacy, "Galen's Platonism", *AJPh*, vol. 93, 1972, pp. 27–39; P. Moraux, "Galien comme philosophe: la philosophie de la nature", in V. Nutton, ed., *Galen: Problems and Prospects*, London: 1981, pp. 87–116; M. Frede, "On Galen's Epistemology", in V. Nutton, pp. 65–86; Pierluigi Donini, *Motivi filosofici in Galeno*, La Parola del Passato, vol. 194, 1980, pp. 333–70.

6 On Galen in the Renaissance, see A. Wear, "Galen in the Renaissance", in V. Nutton 1981, pp. 229–62; J.H. Randall Jr., *The School of Padua and the Emergence of Modern Science*, Padua: 1961; N. Gilbert, *Renaissance Concepts of Method*, New York: 1960.

7 On the Empiricists, see K. Deichgräber, *Die griechische Empirikerschule*, Berlin: 1930; L. Edelstein, "Empiricism and Skepticism in the Teaching of the Greek Empiricist School", in L. Edelstein, *Ancient Medicine*, Baltimore: 1967, pp. 195–208.

8 On the Methodists, see L. Edelstein, "The Methodists", in L. Edelstein, *Ancient Medicine*, Baltimore: 1967, pp. 173–91; M. Frede, "The Method of the So-called Methodical School of Medicine", in *Science and Speculation*, ed. J. Barnes, J. Brunschwig, M. Burnyeat, M. Schofield, Cambridge: 1982, pp. 1–23.

On the Sects for Beginners

On the Sects for Beginners

CHAPTER 1

The aim of the art of medicine is health, but its end is the possession of   1
health. Doctors have to know by which means to bring about health,
when it is absent, and by which means to preserve it, when it is present.
Those things which bring about health when it is not there are called
medicines and remedies; those things which preserve it when it is there,
healthy regimens. Thus it is also that an ancient account says that medicine is the science of what is healthy and of what is unhealthy, calling
healthy those things which preserve an existing health or restore a ruined
health, unhealthy the opposite of these. For the doctor needs the knowledge of both to choose the one and to avoid the other.

But whence one may come by the knowledge of these no longer is
universally agreed upon. Some say that experience alone suffices for the
art, whereas others think that reason, too, has an important contribution
to make. Those who rely on experience [*empeiria*] alone are accordingly
called empiricists. Similarly, those who rely on reason are called rational-   2
ists. And these are the two primary sects in medicine. The one proceeds
by means of experience to the discovery of medicines, the other by
means of indication. And thus they have named their sects empiricist and
rationalist. But they also customarily call the empiricist sect observational

Marginal numbers refer to pages in Helmreich.

3

and relying on memory and the rationalist sect dogmatic and analogistic. And, corresponding to the sects, they call the persons who have chosen to follow experience empiricists, observationists, and those who rely on their memory of phenomena, whereas they call those who have adopted reason rationalists, dogmatics, and analogists.

CHAPTER 2

The empiricists claim that the art comes about in the following way. One has observed many affections in people. Of these, some occur spontaneously, both in the sick and the healthy, e.g., nosebleeding, or sweat, or diarrhea, or something else of the kind which brings harm or advantage, though one cannot see what it is that produced the effect. In the case of other affections, the cause is manifest, but they, too, occur not due to some choice of ours, but somehow by chance. Thus it just so happened that somebody fell or was hit or wounded in some other manner and that, hence, there was a flow of blood, or that somebody who was ill gratified his appetites and drank cold water or wine or something else of the kind, each of which had a harmful or beneficial effect. The first kind of beneficial or harmful event they called natural, the second, chance. But, in both cases, they called the first observation of such an event an incidence, choosing this name because one happens upon these things not on purpose. The incidental kind of experience, then, is roughly like this. The extemporary kind, on the other hand, is characterized by the fact that we deliberately come to try something, either led by dreams or forming a view as to what is to be done in some other fashion. But there is yet a third kind of experience, namely, the imitative one. An experience is imitative if something which has proved to be beneficial or harmful, either naturally or by chance or by extemporization, is tried out again for the same disease. It is this kind of experience which has contributed most to their art. For when they have imitated, not just twice or three times, but very many times, what has turned out to be beneficial on earlier occasions, and when they then find out that, for the most part, it has the same effect in the case of the same diseases, then they call such a memory a theorem and think that it already is trustworthy and forms part of the art. But when many such theorems had been accumulated by them, the whole accumulation amounted to the art of medicine, and the person who had accumulated the theorems, to a doctor. Such an accumulation came to be called by them one's own perception [autopsia]. For what it consists in is a certain kind of memory of what one often has perceived to happen in the same way. But they also called the very same thing experience. History, on the other hand, they called the report of one's own perception. For the very same thing counts as one's own perception for the person who has made the observations, but as history for the person who is learning what has been observed.

Now, it also sometimes happened that one encountered diseases which had not been seen before or diseases which were known, but which one encountered in areas where there was no ready supply of medicines which had been observed by experience. Hence they turned the transition to the similar into some sort of device to find remedies. By means of this device, they often transfer the same remedy from one affection to another and from one place affected to another, and they proceed from a previously known remedy to one quite similar. Thus they might make the transition from one disease to another by going from erysipelas to herpes, from one place affected to another, as from the arm to the thigh, from one remedy to another, as, in the case of diarrhea, from apple to medlar. This kind of transition, as a whole, amounts to a method of invention but not yet to invention itself, before the test has been made. But, once one has put what one expected to the test, it already is trustworthy, if it has been confirmed by this, no less so than if it had been observed many times to happen in the same way. This experience which one has a result of the transition to the similar they call practiced, because one has to be practiced in the art if one wants to find something out in this way. But all the other experiences which were made before one had this kind of experience and which were needed to bring about the art can also be made by anyone. Such, then, is the method which proceeds by means of experience to attain the end of the art.

4

Chapter 3

The method, on the other hand, which proceeds by means of reason admonishes us to study the nature of the body which one tries to heal and the forces of all the causes which the body encounters daily. For it is as a result of these that it becomes healthier or sicker than it was before. Moreover, they say, the doctor also has to be knowledgeable about airs, waters, places, occupations, foods, drinks, and habits, so that he may figure out the causes of all diseases and be able to compare and to calculate the forces of the remedies, i.e., that something which has such and such a force, if applied to this kind of cause, naturally produces that kind of

5

effect. For, they say, it is not possible to have an ample choice of remedies to resort to, unless one has been trained in all these things in their
many aspects. Thus, so that one may gather the whole matter from a
small example, let us assume that some part of the body is in pain, hard,
resistant, and swollen. Here the doctor first of all has to find out the
cause, namely, that some fluid has flowed into the part in an abnormal
amount, has made it swell and, by stretching it, has caused pain. Then, if
the fluid continues to flow in, he has to prevent it from flowing; if it does
not continue, he can already proceed to empty the part affected. How,
then, will one stop the fluid from continuing to flow; how will one empty
out what has been already gathered? By cooling and constricting the part,
one will prevent the inflow; by warming it up and relaxing it, one will
empty it of what has been gathered. Thus the disposition itself offers the
rationalists the indication of what is beneficial. But this indication in itself
is not enough, they say; we also need another indication, derived from
the strength of the patient, and another one, from his age, and yet
another one, from the particular nature of the patient himself. But in this
way, we also obtain a particular indication of what is beneficial from the
seasons of the year, the nature of the place, occupations, and habits. One
may be able to see this, too, more clearly in the case of an example;
hence let us assume that somebody has a high fever and resents movement and his body feels heavy. Let us also assume that he is heavier than
before and that he has more flesh. Moreover, let us assume that his veins
have increased in size. Somehow, it is clear to everybody that such a person has an abundance of blood which is too hot. What, then, is the cure?
Obviously evacuation. For this is what is contrary to abundance, and contraries are the remedies of contraries. How, then, will we empty it out,
and to what extent? This one can no longer know just by knowing the
cause. For one also has to consider the strength, the age, the season, the
place, and all the other things mentioned a little while ago. For if the
patient is strong and in the prime of life, and if it is spring, and if the
place has a moderate climate, then one will not go wrong if one applies
phlebotomy and empties out as much blood as the cause demands. But if
his strength is weak and his age is that of an altogether small child or of a
man in advanced years, and if the place has a cold climate, like the places
in Scythia, or a hot climate, like the places in Ethiopia, and if the season
of the year is very hot or very cold, one will no longer dare to apply phlebotomy. Similarly they also advise to take into consideration habits,
occupations, and the nature of the bodies. For all these things, they say,
provide their proper indication of what is beneficial.

The same things from which the dogmatics draw the indication of what is beneficial form the basis of the observation of the empiricist. For the collection of symptoms mentioned above in the case of the person who has fever, the collection which they are in the habit of calling a syndrome, suggests evacuation to the dogmatic, to the empiricist a recollection of his observation. For, since he has often seen in cases like this that evacuation is beneficial, he expects that it will also prove useful when he uses it now. But he also knows on the basis of what he has often seen that persons, if they are in their prime age, stand the appropriate evacuation without difficulty. Similarly also, if it is spring, rather than summer, and if it is in a place with moderate climate, and if the patient is somewhat accustomed to evacuation, e.g., through hemorrhoids or through nosebleeding. The dogmatic, too, would for this reason draw more blood, but relying in this on the nature of the matter, whereas the empiricist would do it because he has made these observations. And, to speak quite generally, the dogmatics and the empiricists draw on the same medicines for the same affections. What they disagree about is the way these remedies are discovered. For, in the case of the same manifest bodily symptoms, the dogmatics derive from them an indication of the cause, and, on the basis of this cause, they find a treatment, whereas the empiricists are reminded by them of what they have observed often to happen in the same way. But, in those cases in which the dogmatics do not have a manifest symptom which is indicative of the cause, they do not hesitate to ask for the so-called antecedent cause, e.g., whether one was bitten by a mad dog or a snake or something else of the kind. For the wound itself does not look any different from the other wounds, except at the very beginning. For, in the case of the mad dog, the wound throughout looks similar to the wound of someone who has been bitten by something else. In the case of snakes, though, the wound looks similar to the others in the first days, but then, when the patient's state already has deteriorated, some deadly bodily affections present themselves. Such symptoms, which are produced by the so-called venomous animals, are almost invariably fatal, unless they are properly treated right from the start. What, then, is the correct treatment? It is obvious that one has to evacuate the poison which entered the body of the person who was bitten at the time of the bite. Hence one should not encourage scarring and try to close such a wound, but, on the contrary, make a lot of cuts, especially if it is small, and, for the same reason, use hot and pungent drugs which can draw out and dry up the poison. The empiricists, too, apply the same drugs. But they are led not by the nature of the matter itself to the discovery of these drugs,

7

8

but because they remember what has become apparent through their experience. Just as, in the case of age, season, and place, the therapy appropriate for each of the things mentioned is known to them through experience, thus it is also when it comes to the so-called antecedent causes. If, then, they were to grant each other that both methods of invention are correct, they would have no further need for lengthy arguments.

9

CHAPTER 5

But the dogmatists have levelled various criticisms against empiricism. Some have said that this kind of experience is unrealizable, and others, that it is incomplete, while a third group has claimed that it is not technical. The empiricists, on the other hand, have criticized rationalist reasoning as being plausible, but not true. Hence the account which both of them give is twofold and turns out to be rather lengthy, as they raise particular criticisms and defend themselves against them.

Some of these criticisms of empiricism have been raised by Asclepiades. He thought he was able to show that nothing can be seen often to happen in the same way. Hence he thought that this kind of experience was utterly unrealizable and would not be in a position to make possible even the most modest discovery. Other criticisms have been raised by Erasistratus. Erasistratus is willing to grant that simple remedies for simple cases can be found by experience, e.g., that andrachne is a cure against having the teeth set on edge. But he no longer grants this for complex remedies and complex cases. Not that he thinks that experience is utterly incapable of making these discoveries, but that it is not sufficient to find all of them. Finally, those who are willing to grant that these things are found by experience, nevertheless complain about its indefinite, lengthy, and—as they put it—unmethodical character and therefore introduce reason, not because empirical experience is unrealizable or unreal, but because it lacks the character of an art.

10

The empiricists defend themselves against the criticisms and try to show that empirical experience is realizable, that it is sufficient, and that it is technical. And they, in turn, attack the analogistical reasoning of the rationalists in many fashions, so that now the dogmatics have to defend themselves against each of the criticisms raised. For, when the dogmatics claim to know the nature of the body and the origins of all diseases and the forces of medicines, the empiricists join battle with them and discredit all their claims, arguing that they perhaps reach the level of plausibility and likelihood but that they lack any certain knowledge. Sometimes they also grant them their knowledge but then try to show its uselessness, or they grant its usefulness and then argue for its superfluousness.

Generally speaking, it is such matters the empiricists and the dogmatics argue about with each other. But, on each particular point, there is a multitude of particular issues. For example, in their inquiries concerning the discovery of things which are not manifest, one party praises anatomy, indication, and logical theory. For, they claim, these are their instruments in their search for what is not manifest. The empiricists, on the other hand, do not grant that anatomy makes any discoveries or that it would be necessary for the art, even if it did. Furthermore, they do not grant that there is such a thing as indication or that one thing can be known on the basis of another thing, for one has to know all things on the basis of themselves. Nor do they grant that there is such a thing as a sign of something which by its very nature is nonmanifest. Furthermore, they argue that no art has any need for logic. They even go on and criticize the postulates of logic and definition, claiming that there is no such thing as proof, anyway. And then they talk about the fallacious modes of proof which the dogmatics are accustomed to use and in particular about the whole genre of analogisms. And they argue that, since an analogism is not in a position to be used to uncover what it is pretended it can uncover, no art will be realized on the basis of it, nor will human life, on the basis of it, make progress. The epilogism, on the other hand, of which they say that it is a reasoning solely in terms of what is apparent, is of use in the discovery of things which are not manifest temporarily. For this is the way they themselves call things which belong to the class of things perceptible but which have not yet become manifest. But the epilogism also is useful, if one wants to refute those who dare to argue against what is manifest. It is also of use to point out that some phenomenon has been overlooked and to counter sophistical arguments. In reasoning this way, one never departs from what is clear but throughout stays within its limits. The analogism, however, they say, is not like this. It starts from what is apparent but then proceeds to matters which are entirely unclear, and that is why it takes so many forms. For, starting from the same phenomena, it arrives now at one and now at another unobvious conclusion. And, at this point, they bring up the problem of the discord which cannot be settled and which they claim is a sign of the incomprehension of things. This is the language they use: "comprehension" for true and certain knowledge, "incomprehension" for the opposite of the first. And they say that this incomprehension is the cause for the discord which cannot be settled and that the discord, in turn, is a sign of the incompre-

11

12

hension. They point out that it is the disagreement concerning matters which are not manifest which cannot be settled, not the disagreement concerning matters which are manifest. For, in their case, everything, once it is apparent what it is like, confirms those who are right about it and refutes those who are wrong about it. Empiricists and dogmatics engage in innumerous disputes of this kind, and yet they apply the same treatment for the same diseases, at least if they have been properly trained in accordance with their respective sect.

CHAPTER 6

The so-called methodists, however (for this is how they call themselves, saying that not even their dogmatic predecessors could claim to approach the art by a method), seem to me not only to disagree with the ancient sects as to the account of the art but, beyond that, also to change the practice of the art in many respects. They claim that neither the part affected has anything useful to offer towards an indication as to the appropriate treatment, nor the cause, nor the age, nor the season, nor the place, nor the consideration of the strength of the patient, nor his nature, nor his disposition. They also put aside habits, claiming that the indication as to what is beneficial, derived from just the affections themselves, is enough for them, and not even from these, taken as specific particulars, but assuming them to be common and universal. And hence they also call these affections which pervade all particulars "communities". And some of them try to show that all internal diseases are characterized by two communities and a third mixed one, whereas some try to show simply that all diseases are thus characterized. These communities they called "costiveness" and "flux", and they say that each disease is either costive or fluent or a combination of both. For, when the natural bodily outflows are interrupted, one calls this "costive"; when they flow too freely, one calls it "fluent". When they both are interrupted and flow, the combination consists in exactly this, as in the case of the eye which is both inflamed and at the same time running. For the inflammation is a costive affection, but, since it now occurs not by itself but in conjunction with and in the same place as the flux, the whole thing amounts to a combined affection. What is indicated as beneficial in the case of the costive is laxation, in the case of the fluent, constriction. For if, to take an example, a knee is inflamed, they say that one has to relax it; but, if the bowels or the eye is running, one has to stop and to constrict. In the combined condition, one has to counteract the more pressing element. For they say that one has to counter what is more troublesome and what presents the greater danger, rather than the other element.

Why, then, did they not call themselves dogmatics, given that they derive their remedies from indication? Because, they say, the dogmatics search for what is not manifest, while we only occupy ourselves with what is apparent. And, in fact, they define their whole doctrine accordingly as a knowledge of apparent communities, and, to avoid letting the definition be thought to apply to all other arts (for they take these, too, to   14 be knowledge of apparent communities), they add "which are relevant to the end of medicine". Some of them, though, add not "which are relevant" but "which accord". The vast majority combines both and says that the Method is knowledge of apparent communities which accord with and are relevant to the end of medicine, but some, among them Thessalus, add "which are proximate to and necessary for health". It is for this reason that they think they should not be called dogmatics, for, unlike them, they have no need for what is not manifest. But nor yet are they empiricists; since, however much they may occupy themselves with what is apparent, they are separated from the empiricists by their use of indication. They also say that they do not even agree with the empiricists in the manner in which they occupy themselves solely with what is apparent. For, they say, the empiricists will have nothing to do with what is not manifest, claiming that it is unknowable, whereas they themselves will have nothing to do with what is not manifest, because it is useless. Moreover, it is observation which the empiricists derive from what is apparent, whereas they derive an indication from it. They claim to differ from both in these regards, then, and also, most of all, in that they dispense with seasons, places, ages, and all the like, matters which are obviously useless, as they think, but held in high regard by earlier doctors because of their vainglory. And they say that this is the greatest benefit of the methodist sect, they take great pride in it and think they deserve admiration. They scold the man who has said that life is short and the art long. Quite   15 the contrary, they say, the art is short and life is long. For, if one does away with all those things which have been wrongly taken to further the art and if we attend only to the communities, then medicine is neither long nor difficult, but rather is easy and clear and can be learned as a whole in a matter of six months. For, in this way, the whole matter of internal diseases is reduced to a short affair, and similarly with surgery and pharmacology. For there, too, they try to find certain communities which apply universally and assume such a limited number of aims for cures that it seems to me that it would take not even the notorious six months, but much less, to master their whole art. And thus one should recognize one's indebtedness to them for such a concise doctrine, if, that is, they are not wrong. But if they are wrong, one has to criticize their lack of seriousness.

CHAPTER 7

I will now try to say how I think one would best arrive at a fair judgment as to whether they are just blind as to what is useful or whether they alone rightly avoid what is superfluous. This seems to be a question of no small importance. For, unlike the dogmatics and the empiricists, whose sole contention is over the first discovery of our remedies, whereas they agree with each other on their present use, the methodists seem to me to go beyond mere argument. Hence the practice of the art will necessarily either suffer great damage or be greatly advanced by the methodist sect. Now, there are two ways to judge matters. One way proceeds by argument alone; the other goes by what is clearly apparent. The first, which proceeds by argument alone, is beyond mere beginners. Hence this is not the right occasion for it. The other one, which goes by what is apparent, is the way commonly followed by everybody. Why, then, should we not use this method first, given that it is both clear to beginners and held in high regard by the methodists themselves? For invariably they sing the praise of what is apparent and pay honour to it on every occasion, whereas they say of all that is not manifest that it is useless.

Let us, then, first consider the matter of the so-called antecedent causes, taking as our standard of judgment what is apparent. And let us assume that the methodist steps up first and speaks roughly in the following way: Why, dogmatists and empiricists, do you vainly concern yourselves at such length with chills, burns, drunkenness, indigestions, excesses, deficiencies, toils, idleness, the qualities of foods, and changes of habits? It is these matters, rather than the bodily dispositions, which you want to cure, matters which are not even present anyway but have passed away, though their effect remains in the body, and it is this which one has to cure. For this is the affection. Hence one has to look at it to see what it is like. If it is costive, one has to relax it; if it is fluent, one has to constrict it, whatever the cause for either disposition may be. Of what use, then, is the cause, given that the fluent should never be relaxed and the costive never be constricted? Obviously of no use, as the matter itself shows.

What the methodists have to say about about the so-called containing causes which are nonmanifest is similar. For they say that these, too, are superfluous, since the affection itself indicates the proper treatment, and

this without our knowledge of the cause through which it came about. They proceed to use the same kind of arguments in the case of seasons, places, and ages, wondering here, too, about the ancient doctors, whether they really do not grasp such an obvious matter. For an inflamed tumour, they say, is a costive affection. Hence it is not the case that it needs laxative remedies if it should happen to be in summer but some other remedies in winter, but rather it needs the same remedies in both seasons. Nor do we need laxatives if we deal with the age of a child but constrictives when we deal with the age of the elderly, nor laxatives in Egypt but inhibitives in Athens. In the case of the fluent affection, the reverse is true of what obtains in the case of an inflamed tumour. The fluent affection never needs laxatives but always constrictives, in winter, in spring, in summer, in fall, and whether the patient be a child, in the prime of life, or old, and whether he happens to be in Thracia, in Scythia, or in Ionia. Hence, they say, none of these factors is of any use, but all are a matter of idle concern. And what about the parts of the body? Are not these, too,   18
useless for an indication of the treatment? Or would somebody dare to say that an inflamed tumour in the sinewy parts needs laxation, but in an arterial or venous or fleshy part constriction? And quite generally, would anybody dare to say that, if there is costiveness in some part of the body, then it should not be relaxed, or that fluency should not be constricted? If, then, the nature of the part in no way modifies the manner of treatment, but one always finds one's remedies by looking at the kind of the affection, consideration of the part is useless. This, in rough outline, is the kind of position the methodist takes.

Chapter 8

After him, let the empiricist come forward and say something like this: I do not know anything which goes beyond what is apparent, nor do I profess anything more wise than what I have seen oftentimes. If you have no regard for what is apparent, as I think I once heard from some sophist, then it is time for us to go to those who do respect what is apparent, and you can win your Cadmean victory. But if you do say, as I also have heard from you in the beginning, that all that is not manifest is useless and if you agree to follow what is obvious, then, perhaps, I can point out to you what it is that you are overlooking, reminding you of what is apparent.

Two men, bitten by a mad dog, went to their familiar doctors, asking to be cured. In both cases, the wound was small, so that the skin was not

19 even entirely torn, and one of them only treated the wound, not busying himself with anything else, and, after a few days, the part affected seemed to be fine. But the other, since he knew that the dog was mad, far from hastening to have the wound scar, did exactly the opposite and tried constantly to enlarge it, using strong and sharp drugs, till, after a considerable amount of time, he also forced the patient at this point to drink the medicines appropriate for madness, as he himself explained. And this is the end the whole matter took in both cases. The one who drank the medicines was saved and became healthy again. The other thought that he was not suffering anything, but all of a sudden came to fear water, went into spasms, and died. Do you think that, in such cases, one inquires in vain into the antecedent cause and that the man died for any other reason than the negligence of the doctor, who failed to ask at all about the cause and to apply the treatment observed in this case? To me it seems that he died for no other reason than this.

But since I follow what is apparent, I cannot pass over any cause of this kind. Similarly, I cannot overlook or disregard the age. For here, too, appearances force me to trust that the same affections do not indicate always the same treatment but at times a treatment which is so different
20 for the different ages that it varies not only in the quantity of the remedy and its manner of application, but altogether in kind. Thus I have seen many people who were in their prime and strong who suffered from pleurisy and who were treated by phlebotomy, often even by yourselves. But not even you yourselves or anybody else has ever dared to let blood in the case of a very old person or a quite small child.

When Hippocrates says, "During and before the dog days, medicines cause problems" or when he says elsewhere, "In summer the upper parts respond better to medication, in winter the lower parts", do you think he is right or wrong? I think you will have a problem answering this either way. For, if you should say that he is wrong, you disregard what is apparent, which you pretend to hold in such regard. For the truth appears to be just like Hippocrates says. But if you should say that he is right, then you do let in seasons, which you claimed are useless. I also think that you never travel far from home and have no experience of the difference between places. Otherwise you would well know that people in the north do not stand concentrated bloodlettings well, nor do those in Egypt and in the south as a whole, whereas those in the region in between these often draw obvious benefit from phlebotomy.

21 That you do not even consider the parts of the body seems to me to be a rather strange thing for you to say and indeed quite absurd, since it runs counter not only to what is true but also to your own practice. By God, is it true that, wherever there is an inflammation, it requires the

same treatment, whether it be in the leg, or the ear, or the mouth, or the eyes? Why, in that case, have I seen you often treat inflammations in the leg by lancing with a knife and then soaking with olive oil, whereas I have never seen you treat eyes this way? Why do you cure inflamed eyes with constringents, and do not also annoint the legs with the same medications? Why do you not also cure inflamed ears with the remedies for eyes, why not also the eyes with the remedies for ears? Instead there is one drug for ear inflammation and another one for eye inflammation. For vinegar with rose oil is a good medicine against inflammation of the ears, but I do not think that anybody would dare to apply it to inflamed eyes. And even if he should dare to do it, I know well that he will have to pay dearly for his daring. And when the uvula is inflamed, a good drug is the fruit of the Egyptian thorn; similarly, fissile alum is good. Are these, then, also good for inflamed eyes and ears, or would they not be, quite the contrary, extremely harmful?

And I am saying all this, granting to you the first assumption, namely, that one has to relax an inflammation in the legs or in the hands, but not that one has to relax an inflammation of the eyes, the uvula, or the ears. And if I remind you that even an inflammation in the legs or the hands should not under all circumstances be relaxed, you perhaps will recognize, if you are reasonable, the extent of your errors. But the present argument, too, will just be a reminder of what is apparent. For when somebody suffers from an inflammation in any part, which is not due to some lesion but which came about by itself, because of the so-called condition of abundance, nobody will apply relaxation to the part before having evacuated the whole body. For one not only would not ameliorate the present inflammation but would increase it, if one did that. Hence, in a situation like this, we will apply astringents and things which cool to the part affected, and only when we have evacuated the whole body, then the inflamed part will also withstand laxatives. But if I do not manage to convince you by what I say, then, as I said in the beginning of my discourse, it should be time for me to leave and to go to those who respect what is apparent.

22

CHAPTER 9

After the empiricist has said this, let the dogmatist come in and give a speech of this kind: If you are not out of your mind, even what has just been said, namely, that one should not assume that age, season, place, or even the antecedent cause or the part of the body are useless, should suffice. But in case the empiricist has not managed to convince you by reminding you of what is apparent and the matter also needs some reasoning, I think I will supply this, and I will show that the assumption on which your sect is based is unsound. For I hear you talk of knowledge of apparent communities, but, when I ask each time about what the community consists in and how we are to recognize it, I never seem to be able, up to the present point, to understand. The reason is this: As far as words go, you agree with each other, but on the matter itself you are in disagreement. For some of you measure the costive and the fluent by the natural secretions; if they are held back, they call the affection "costiveness"; when they are secreted beyond the proper measure, they call it "flux". But others among you, and not a small group, claim that the affections consist in the dispositions of the body themselves, and they harshly criticize those who look towards what is secreted. Perhaps I may explain now how both of them seem to me to be in error. But let me address my words first to those who judge the affections by the natural secretions. In their case, I wonder whether they have never seen in cases of illness that sweat, urine, vomit, and feces were discharged in an unnaturally large amount, but to the benefit of the patient, and, what is most peculiar of all, whether they have never seen how nosebleeding brought a disease to a crisis. For, in the case of nosebleeding, it is not just the quantity of the bleeding but any bleeding itself which is against nature. Sweat, urine, and what is discharged through the stomach or by vomiting, on the other hand, are not by their very kind against nature, but their amount at times is so immoderate that I myself have seen people who sweated so much that their pillows were soaked and others who evacuated more than thirty kotylai through their stomach, and yet I did not decide to stop this, because it was what caused the pain that was discharged. But, if one uses the natural secretions as one's canon in every case, then one would have to stop symptoms of this kind.

Hence it seems to me that they are more persuasive who postulate that the communities are the dispositions in the bodies themselves. But I also wonder, in their case, how they could dare to call them apparent. For, if the flux is not what flows from the cavity of the body but rather the disposition of the bodies in virtue of which there is flux and if this disposition itself cannot become manifest to any of the senses, how could the communities still be apparent? For the disposition of flux can be in the colon, or in the small intestines, or around the intestinum jejunum, the stomach, the mesentery membrane, or lots of other internal parts, none of which one can grasp by perception, either itself or its affection. How, then, can one still talk of apparent communities, unless one also were to say that, if something is being recognized through signs, it is apparent?

But if this is so, I no longer know where there still is a disagreement with the ancient doctors. And how can they claim to teach the art in six months? For they would need, I think, a method of considerable power to recognize something which escapes perception. Somebody who is to do this right, it would rather seem, would need the kind of anatomy which teaches, concerning each of the natural parts, what its natural state is, and one would need no small amount of physical theory, so that he can consider the function and the use of each part. For, unless one has ascertained these matters concerning the parts hidden in the depth of the body, one will not be able to diagnose the affection of any of them. It hardly has to be pointed out that there also is a great need for logic, so that one has a clear idea of what follows from what and is never misled by sophisms, either by somebody else or by oneself. For it also does happen at times that one unknowingly deceives oneself by fallacious reasoning.

Moreover, I would like to ask them what kind of thing flux is, if they have learnt their logic. For I do not think that what some of them have said is sufficient, namely, that flux is some kind of unnatural disposition. For, if we do not learn what kind of disposition it is, we will still not yet know whether it is some kind of relaxation or softness or looseness of texture. For one also cannot find this out from them, given that they say nothing definite but just whatever comes to their mind, now this, now something else, often also everything at once, as if it did not make any difference. And if one tries to inform them how these things differ from each other and how each of them needs its own specific treatment, they not only do not want to hear any of it but even attack the ancients, saying that they made such distinctions for no purpose. So little are they willing to take pains when it comes to the search of the truth. They cannot even bear to hear that the opposite of the relaxed is the tense; of the soft, the hard; of the loose, the dense; and that the interruption of the natural secretions and their flux which are influenced by all these states in each case amount to something different; and that all this has already been distinguished by Hippocrates. But they make rash assertions, both about these matters and about inflammation. An inflammation they call a hard, resistant, painful, and hot swelling, claiming rather readily and without due consideration that it is a costive affection. Then, on another occasion, they call other inflammations mixed, as, for example, eye inflammations, when they involve a flux, or inflammations of the tonsils, the uvula, the roof of the mouth, or the gums. Then they postulate pores, some of which have been dilated, whereas others have been closed, and which, as a result, suffer both affections. Some do not even hesitate to claim that one and the same pore is affected by flux and costiveness, which it is not easy even to imagine. Thus they know no limit in their daring. A few among them, though, are better able to stand listening to objections on all these matters and to consider them thoroughly, as a result of which they change their mind, though rarely, and turn to what is more like the truth. For these and for all those who want to find out about the first and most generic affections in some detail, I have written a special treatise. But here it is appropriate to address at least a few remarks to them, since it is of use for beginners. But I would hope that they, too, derive some benefit from these remarks. This might come about, if they stopped being contentious and examined the argument for themselves. The argument runs like this: What even they themselves call an inflammation is an unnatural painful, resistant, hard, hot swelling which does not, of its own account, make the part affected a bit looser, or denser, or harder, but rather makes it full of superfluous fluid and thus stretched. But it is not universally the case that, if something is stretched, it thereby becomes denser or harder. One may gather this in the case of hides, leather straps, or braids of hair, if one tries to stretch them thoroughly. Thus, too, the cure for things which are repleted consists in their evacuation. For this is the opposite of repletion. But when things are emptied, they as a result become more relaxed in their parts. Tension is a necessary consequence of being repleted, just as relaxation is a consequence of being emptied, but densification or rarefaction do not follow necessarily, nor do flux or interruption of the flow. For it is not the case, either, if a part is loose or rarefied, that it is also necessary under any circumstances that something should flow from it. For what if the matter contained is thick and small in quantity? Nor does it follow that, if it is dense, the flow will be contained. For what comes in a large amount and is thin also runs out through pores which are dense or narrow. Hence it would be better if they, too, read the books of the ancients and learned in how many ways that which first is contained in a part later is secreted. For this happens not only when that which contains it becomes looser but also when that which is contained becomes thinner and grows in amount, or when it is moved too rapidly, or when it is attracted by something on the outside or pushed by something on the inside and, as it were, is sucked up again. If somebody were to pass all these cases over and to believe that there is a single cause for evacuation, namely, the looseness of the pores, he would seem not even to know the phenomena. For we see clearly that, if wool or a sponge or something else which is loose in this way has a small amount of fluid inside it, it contains it and does not give it off, though it sheds what is in excess. Why, then, have they not noticed the very same phenomenon in the case of eyes and nostrils and the mouth and the other parts which are loose in this way, namely, that it might occasionally be in virtue of the

considerable amount of fluid contained in them rather than in virtue of
the looseness of the pores that something flows off? We also often see
earthenware jars which are so loose in texture that water penetrates
them. But if one pours some honey in, it does not penetrate, for the substance of honey is too thick for the pores of the jar. It would not have
been amiss also to take notice of the fact that often something flows off
because of its thinness, even if the containing body itself should not be
perforated by nature. Nor is it difficult for someone who is thoroughly
familiar with the practice of the art to take notice of the fact that nature,
which governs the animal, often uses an unusually strong commotion to
empty it of all that is superfluous, as if she had squeezed it out and
rejected it. For in general the crises of illnesses come about in this way.   29
And I pass over the remaining causes for evacuation and similarly those
for congestion, which are equal in number, since they are just the contraries of the first. For this kind of argument is not the appropriate instruction for that audience. Rather I will return to what I think they might just
be able to understand, namely, that there can be a flow from the eye,
either because there is a lot of fluid which has gathered, because it has
become thin, or because it is pushed out by nature through this part,
even if the bodies themselves are no more in an abnormal state just
because of this. And obviously one has to thicken the fluid which is thin
and evacuate what is abundant. But the natural commotion one should
not interfere with, if it sets in opportunely, and one should not occupy
oneself with the bodies of the eyes themselves, since they are not respon-
sible for the flux. But I do not understand how it can be reasonable to
think that one kind of inflammation is a costive affection, whereas
another kind is mixed. For, first of all, they do not mind their own
accounts, according to which one should not judge the fluent by the evacuation or the costive by the interruption of flux, but should look at the
dispositions of the bodies themselves. Where, then, the present inflama-
tion happens to be similar in all respects to the previous one and where
they appear to differ in no other way than that in one case something
flows off, whereas in the other it does not, how is it not completely
absurd to take the one to be mixed and the other to be costive? Secondly,
how is it that they also were not able to figure out what must have been
all too obvious, namely, that one has never seen, either in a hand, a foot,   30
a forearm, an arm, the lower leg, the thigh, or some other bodily part, the
kind of inflammation which involves some discharge, and that this characterizes only inflammation in the mouth and the eyes and the nose?
Could the reason be that Zeus gave all mixed communities the order that
none of them should ever visit any other bodily part, but only wage war
on the eyes, the nose, and the mouth? For inflammation can overcome

whatever allows by its nature for the causes of its coming into being. But, since some things by nature are loose in texture, whereas others are dense, some of the fluid flows off in one case, whereas it is contained in the other. For, if one fills a skin or some other container of this kind with a fluid substance, nothing flows off, whereas, if one fills a sponge or some other thing which is loose in this way, all the excess fluid is shed immediately. Why, then, is it so difficult for them to realize how much more all the other kinds of skin are capable of retaining fluids than the skins of the eyes, the nostrils, and the mouth, and to ascribe the cause to the nature of the parts involved, giving up on mixed states and lengthy gibberish. For it is clear that this is how things are, from the inflammations which occur in conjunction with ulceration in the other parts. For, in their case, too, what is rather thin flows off, just as in the case of eyes, nose, and mouth. But so long as the skin is not affected and still holds things completely in, the reason nothing flows off is exactly this, and not the nature of the inflammation. If one puts honey or raw pitch, in an amount which is not quite out of proportion, on sponge or wool, nothing flows off, because of the thickness of the fluid; or if one puts on water or some other equally thin liquid, but in a very small amount, again nothing will flow off in their case, because of the small amount of the fluid. Similarly, I think, for the same reason, it is not under any circumstances that there is a discharge from the eyes, either because of the thickness of the fluid or because there is no excess; this is just the case of eyes which are in a natural state. Thus it is possible that an inflammation which does not differ from another inflammation in anything but the thickness of the fluid which collects should produce ophthalmia which is not accompanied by a flux, but which these ever so wise methodists call a costive affection and which they think essentially differs from the mixed condition, not minding their own accounts, which they shift around all the time, according to which they postulate that the states characteristic of the affections are bodily states and are not constituted by the states of the fluids. How, then, can it be assumed that the communities are different, when the disposition in the bodies does not differ at all, except that it follows upon the nature of the fluids, because they are thin or thick, that in one case something flows off and in the other the fluid is contained. Thus the mixed state which you postulate is unintelligible, too. As to all the other points of detail, not only in matters of internal diseases, but also in matters of surgery and pharmacy, perhaps you will learn another time on how many things you are in error, if you are not already persuaded by these arguments. But, since just these are sufficient for the beginners, I will thus conclude my present account here.

An Outline of Empiricism

An Outline of Empiricism

CHAPTER I

Introductory, on Galen's intention in this book

All doctors who are followers of experience, just like the philosophers who are called Sceptics, refuse to be called after a man, but rather want to be known by their frame of mind. And accordingly they say that, though the other doctors are called Hippocratics or Erasistrateans or Praxagoreans or Asclepiadeans or by some other name of this kind, they themselves are not called Acronians (though Acron was the first representative of empirical doctrines), nor yet after Timon, or after Philinus, or Serapion, men who came after Acron, but were earlier than the rest of the empiricists. In this, then, they all agree. But, in addition, he will be the most reliable exponent of empiricism who refrains, in whatever he says, from claiming any of those things which are thought to be found out only by indicative inference. For they want to say that the art of medicine is constituted, not by indicative inference in conjunction with experience, as all dogmatic doctors claim, but rather solely by the experience of those things which have been found to happen for the most part and in a similar way. With this in mind, then, judge each of the things said,

43

Marginal numbers refer to pages in Deichgräber.

while I will put forth precisely what kind of doctrine it is which characterizes the empiricist position. But let us suppose that the person who
says all the things which are to be found in this book himself is an empiricist.

44   CHAPTER II

which explains whence the art of
medicine, according to the empiricists, has
taken its origin

We say that the art of medicine has taken its origin from experience, and
not from indication. By "experience", we mean the knowledge of something which is based on one's own perception, by "indication", the
knowledge which is based on rational consequence. For perception leads
us to experience, whereas reason leads the dogmatics to indication.
Knowledge based on one's own perception sometimes comes about
spontaneously when one happens to see something, and it is called "incidence". Sometimes, though, it comes about either when one extempo-
rizes or when one imitates something one has already seen. Those cases
of knowledge are said to come about spontaneously which come about
by chance or by nature; by chance, as when somebody who has a pain in
the back of his head happens to fall, cuts the right vein on his forehead,
45   loses blood, and gets better; by nature, or naturally, as when somebody
starts to have nosebleeding and then loses his fever. An extemporary
experience comes about when, for example, somebody gets better
because of his craving to drink cold water or to eat a pomegranate or a
pear or something else of this sort or when it occurs to somebody who
has been bitten by some beast in the mountains to apply such and such
an herb, and he gets better as a result. An imitative experience we gain
when it is seen that something works in a certain way and when it is also
seen that things already have worked this way before, twice or three
times or often, but not so often that one is in a position to say whether
this result always comes about, if this is applied to that, or whether this
result appears only most of the time, half of the time, or rarely. Practiced,
i.e., learned experience, on the other hand, is only to be had by experts
when they are guided by the similarity with things which already have
been found out by experience. By "experience" [*empeiria*], we mean the
knowledge of those things which have become apparent so often that
they already can be formulated as theorems, i.e., when it is known

whether they always have turned out this way, or only for the most part, or half of the time, or rarely. These are the four differentiations of theorems. Hence we will also say that a theorem is the knowledge of something which has been seen often but a knowledge which involves at the same time a distinct knowledge of results to the contrary. This will be a distinction between what happens always (as something whose contrary never makes its appearance), what happens for the most part (as something whose contrary does appear, but rarely), what happens either way, as it may chance be (as something whose contrary appears equally often), and finally what happens rarely (because its contrary does appear, not just sometimes, but for the most part). But those things for which we do not have this kind of distinction, we say, are unordered, and the knowledge of them is not really a part of experience. Menodotus called this kind of experience particular experience, and he said that it was not composed out of other particular experiences and hence was first and most simple.

46

Chapter III

*which explains in which way the parts of
medicine are acquired, i.e., one's own
perception, history, the transition to the
similar, imitation, practiced, spontaneous,
and extemporary observation, yet not all
of these things are touched upon here, but
only some of them*

Just as the whole of the art consists of more than one experience, thus each of these experiences, in turn, consists of many experiences. But the question on how many it rests does not allow of a definite answer and is subject to the kind of puzzle some call a sorites. This puzzle is discussed in more detail in another book entitled "On Medical Experience".

47

In the ancient Greek authors, I have found the word "somebody-who-has-seen-for-himself" [autoptes], but I have not found the word "one's-own-perception" [autopsia]. But, just as we proceed in other cases in this way, so here, too, we coin a derivative term and speak of one's own perception. But somebody's perceiving something for himself consists of an activity and not a cognition. Yet earlier empiricists are in the habit of speaking of one's own perception not only as an activity but also as a cognition, and, what is more, they even used "experience" itself this way.

And we, too, will follow their usage in this respect, and thus we will call not only every cognition of what is apparent but also the experience

48   which is built up from many such cognitions one's own perception. But, for reasons I do not know, they are in the habit of using the term "observation" as equivalent to "cognition" and to "memory of what has been found out". And this is also the reason Theodas says that we acquire the parts of medicine, through which we, by and large, reach our aim, by experience, which comes about through one's own perception, through history and through transition based on correspondence, and then, in defining the kind of experience which does not differ at all from one's own perception, goes on to say that one therefore calls an experience any observation of what has become manifest. Here he uses "observation", instead of which one also speaks of "conservation", in the sense of memory and cognition, though an observation is an activity of something which observes, and though this term, strictly speaking, does not signify a memory or a cognition.

These words, then, the empiricists have not used in accordance with
49   Greek usage. But the word "practice" they have used just like the Greeks did. For it is the practical applications of experience that lie in activity which they call "practice". It is after this that the person who takes part in it is also called a "practician" by the Greeks, just as the person who has experience is called an "empiricist". The Greeks did not use to use the term "empiricist", but those who founded empiricism call themselves "empiricists". For they call "experience" not only the cognition of some particular theorem but the whole of medicine, of which they say that it consists of the experience of what one has perceived for oneself (which they call one's own perception), along with history and the transition to the similar. By "history", they mean the report of one's own perception; by "transition to the similar", a method which leads to practical experience which is based on the similarity with what one already knows by experience.

Chapter IV

*On the transition to the similar, and on
history by way of an inquiry, and on the
characterization of experience*

The question has been raised whether Serapion, too, believes that the transition to the similar is a third constitutive part of the whole of medicine. Menodotus taught that it was not, but that the empiricist makes use only of the transition to the similar. But it is not the same thing to make use of something and to treat it as a part. The Pyrrhonean Cassius, furthermore, tries to show that the empiricist does not even make use of this kind of transition; indeed, he has written a whole book on this matter. Theodas did better when he said that transition by similarity constituted reasonable experience. Yet others, though, have claimed that transition to the similar is more like an instrument. But perhaps it is better to say of history, too, that it is, as it were, an instrument, rather than a part of medicine. But, in this case, it would also be better if one spoke of observation, of which I have already said that it rather is an activity, in this way, too.

It is for this reason, it seems to me, that Theodas himself wrote about these matters in this way: We obtain the parts of medicine, through which we reach our aim, by experience, which, in turn, comes about through one's own observation, through history, and through the kind of transition which is based on correspondence. When he says that it is through these that we obtain the parts of medicine, he obviously thinks that the parts of medicine are something different from these means and that they, generally speaking, are a kind of memory. And, because of this, it is more appropriate if one characterizes experience as the memory of what one has seen to happen often and in the same way. But, if one uses the terms "observation" and "memory" interchangeably, experience then will also be the observation of those things one has often seen. But, if one uses the term "observation" for the activity, as indeed the Greeks do use it, and the term "memory" for the fact that one has kept in mind what one has seen, then one can combine both and say that experience is the observation and the memory of those things which one has seen to happen often and in a similar way, or one can just say that it is the memory of these things. For observation is already implicit in memory, since we cannot remember those things which have been seen to happen often and in a similar way, unless we in some way make their observation.

Chapter V

*on the parts of medicine according to the
empiricists; they are three: semiotics,
therapeutics, and hygiene*

I thought it would be good to give a concise account of these. Theodas
assumed that the whole of medicine has three parts: semiotics, therapeutics, and the so-called hygiene. We acquire these, he says, on the basis of
our own perception, history, and the transition to the similar. And
because of this, those who call these things parts of the whole of experience do not call them this without any further addition, just saying that
they are parts, but they rather say that these are constitutive parts, i.e.,
the parts which constitute the whole of medicine, whereas they say that
semiotics, therapeutics, and hygiene are the final parts of the whole of
medicine, thus contradistinguishing final and constitutive parts. But those
who want to characterize the matter properly do not take these to be
52   parts of medicine at all but rather to be certain activities of the doctor. It
is rather the knowledge in the soul, in accordance with which the doctor
makes inferences from signs, and heals, and takes care of the healthy,
which is a part of medicine. But often they express themselves the other
way, using language loosely. And we, too, follow their usage, and we say
that these are the parts of the whole of medicine: semiotics, therapeutics,
and hygiene. Semiotics has for its parts the diagnosis of what is present
and the prognosis of what is to come. To therapeutics belong surgery,
dietetics, and pharmacology. Here we have to remember that they use
the same terms to refer both to the activities and to the bodies of knowledge on the basis of which we act. Hygiene some keep undivided. But
others divide it into a more specifically hygienic part and into a part concerned with the good shape of the body, whereas others have added to
this a prophylactic, a restorative, and a gerontological part, i.e., one which
guides the old. Yet there are others who say that, though these are all
subdivisions of the whole of medicine, these subdivisions are a result of
the division of what is neither healthy nor unhealthy, as opposed to what
is healthy and to what is unhealthy; and this division of what is neither
they want to be threefold: into bodies, causes, and signs. Herophilus too,
53   made this assumption and said that the whole of medicine consists of the
knowledge of what is healthy, of what is neither, and of what is
unhealthy. But what is neither healthy nor unhealthy is also to be found
both among signs and among causes. It makes good sense to divide the
matter in this way, to be in a better position to teach what is thus divided,
as long as we preserve the empiricist attitude. But I do not object if others

divide things in a different way, so long as no subdivision of the art gets left out by the division. For this reason Theodas, too, at the beginning of his exposition of the parts, has this to say: its parts, i.e., semiotics, therapeutics, and the so-called hygiene, one has to say, also allow for a division into other parts. Thus it is no longer surprising if some have said that experience is made up of two bodies of doctrine; others, of three; others, of four; and yet others, of five. For they themselves say that this amounts not to a disagreement but only to a difference in words, as if they meant that there was one doctrine which just was worded differently. But which division it is which reason would dictate will be said shortly.

Chapter VI

in which he first explains illness and symptoms and then deals with the distinction or determination which one makes in the constitutive parts of medicine, which are diagnostic, prognostic, and therapy

Let us again talk of the constitutive parts of medicine, at least of those which have not yet been discussed. They are the most useful of all: The doctor who just relies on observation has called himself an empiricist and the whole of the art, experience. In the beginning, as is reasonable, he observed what is beneficial and what is harmful, not only among things which it is useful to observe but also among those which it is useless to observe. In the course of the long time down to the present, though, with a multitude of observers having observed a vast array of things, many things have been found to have been observed in vain. And, for this reason, it is now history which is most useful, while earlier it was one's own perception. For one has observed that the colour of clothes in many diseases is of no use, whereas in a few it is useful. For somebody who suffers from ophthalmia is helped by the colours blue, green, and black, whereas a light and gleaming colour is most adverse, and other colours are somewhere in the middle between both. In the same way, it has been observed that a red colour exacerbates those who spew blood, while, with other diseases and symptoms, the observation of this colour has turned out to be useless and superfluous; just as whether a table is ivory or wooden or a flask is made of gold, silver, or glass. For none of these is conducive to health or to illness, but they are neither and, so, superfluous. If something, on the other hand, displays a horrible or obnoxious odour, it is neither superfluous nor neutral, so far as health is concerned. For things which have a bad odour undermine the appetitive and the digestive power. Harm is done to these by things which are strong in their qualities, such as cypress, black poplar, boxwood, and nut tree, especially if they are fresh. Hence we avoid a bed, a door, and a vessel of any kind made from such wood and similarly any odour which fills the head and weakens the appetite or has some other such effect. For, just as it is useful to choose what is beneficial, so it is useful to avoid what is harmful. But what is neither, one does not have to choose or to avoid. And for this reason it is necessary that a doctor be knowledgeable about these things, i.e., about what is healthy, what is unhealthy, and what is neither, not only in the case of causes but also in those of bodies and of signs. But it does not make any difference whether one uses "to have knowledge" or "to be aware of", just as it does not make any difference whether one uses "to be a craftsman" or "to be knowledgeable", or "to

56   learn an art" or "to learn a science". It also does not make any difference whether one says that an inflamed tumour, just to take an example, is an illness or an affection. But it is something different to speak of a symptom, for a symptom is one simple thing and not a composite or aggregate of many things. A side ache is a symptom, and so is a cough, and so is bloody or yellow or livid spit; no less a symptom is shortness of breath and, similarly, unnatural warmth. But the aggregate of all these things the Greeks call an illness or an affection but also a pain or an infirmity. But we use terms, as far as we can, in accordance with Greek usage or, if this cannot be ascertained, then in accordance with some mutual agreement. It will then be good enough, if, for the purposes of clear communication or teaching and learning, one calls a symptom what, among things which are unnatural, is one without qualification (be it a color, a growth, an

57   inflammation, shortness of breath, a cold, a pain, or a cough) and if a syndrome of these is called an affection or an illness. For this is what all empiricists before us have called such a combination. But they did not call just any aggregate of symptoms this, but only when the symptoms arise in the body of the patient simultaneously and if they simultaneously grow, come to a halt, decline, and dissolve. Thus, for the sake of concise exposition, they have decided on a certain term for each syndrome, calling them differently after different items involved in the syndrome. Thus, for example, they call pleurisy and pneumonia after the part which is affected; an inflamed tumour and phrenesis, after a symptom; sometimes they call a syndrome after some similarity, as in the case of elephantiasis and cancer; sometimes they make the whole name up for

themselves, as with edema and scirrhus. Those affections which arise and
grow at the same time and which come to a halt and decline and disap-   58
pear simultaneously they call "coinvadentia", whereas those which only
usually go together are called "constituents". Of the syndromes themselves, some point to a diagnosis of the affection, and they are called
"diagnostic"; others indicate what is going to happen in the future, and
they are called "prognostic"; yet others are suggestive of a kind of treatment, and they are called "therapeutic". But all these syndromes we
know on the basis of observation; we commend them to our memory and
then make use of them on the basis of our recollection. For we make use
of our experience, observing things and trying to remember what we
have seen to happen in conjunction with what, and what we have seen
following what, and what we have seen preceding what, and whether this
is always so, for the most part, half of the time, or rarely. Always, as
death in the case of a heart wound; for the most part, as purgation from
the use of scammony resin; half of the time, as death in the case of a
lesion of the dura mater; rarely, as health in the case of a cerebral wound.
Finally, in all these cases, it is necessary to determine what is peculiar to
the particular case and to distinguish it from what is common, following
in this the constitution of the art, which we bring about by observation
and memory, and, moreover, the exposition of its constitution. Most   59
empiricists if not all, call this a distinction and not a determination, being
well aware, though, of the pride they take in their attitude concerning
matters of nomenclature. In line with this, we will say that it does not
make any difference which of the two expressions one uses, so long as
one does distinguish what is peculiar from what is common. But one
should follow Plato's advice not to take words seriously but not to neglect the exactness of accounts. For it is necessary that one should distinguish what is peculiar from what is common. In diagnosing a disease, one
does this in the following way: If somebody should ask to which illness
the combination of an acute fever with shortness of breath and coughing
and colored saliva belongs, we will answer that the aforementioned combination is common to pleurisy and to pneumonia, but that it is not complete for either case but is lacking in something and truncated. But, if one
adds to the symptoms mentioned above, a sharp side ache and a hard
and punctuated pulse, accompanied by tension, the disease will be pleu-   60
risy. But, if there is no side ache and the pulse is not hard, but the person
can breathe only in an upright posture and has a feeling of constriction,
so that he thinks he is suffocating, such a syndrome is called pneumonia.

   In this way, then, one makes a distinction in the diagnosis of diseases,
which they also callsemeiosis between what is common and what is
peculiar in each particular case. In prognosis, one proceeds this way: If

somebody should ask what a sharp nose, hollow eyes, and sunken temples indicate for the future, we will say that, in the case of a very chronic disease, these symptoms signify some moderate damage, but if they occur at the outset of an illness, they indicate the danger of imminent death. This, then, is the first determination, the one from the stage of the illness. Another determination is derived from what has happened earlier, e.g., when somebody had strong evacuations, but not because of diarrhea or some purgative drug or something else, or when somebody suffered from sleeplessness or hunger. In treatment, one distinguishes what is common from what is peculiar in this way: Should somebody who suffers from pleurisy be treated by phlebotomy? We will say that not everybody should be cut, but only he who has the so-called pleuritic syndrome or, if not this, still is strong and young, and yet not all these, either. For, if somebody has the pleuritic syndrome but is old or an infant, we will refrain from phlebotomy. Similarly, he who lives in a very cold region, e.g., in Scythia, or he who finds himself in the hottest time of summer, during which we have seen many to suffer from a sudden loss of strength, should not be treated by phlebotomy. But this by itself does not yet suffice. For there are yet other determinations besides these: If the pain reaches the collarbone, we will rather use phlebotomy but if it reaches the hypochondrium, we will use purgation.

CHAPTER VII

*in which, to conclude the remarks made
in the preceding chapter about the
determination, he gives its definition and,
furthermore, talks about the difference
between the syndrome of the empiricists
and the syndrome of the dogmatics and
how they differ in the terms they each use
and in their account of the causes*

Such, then, is the determination of a thing. They characterize it by saying that it is an account which distinguishes what is peculiar in each particular case from all those things which are common. But they call it, as I have said, not a determination, but a distinction. To us, however, it will make no difference whether somebody wants to call it a determination or a distinction, so long as the distinction between the syndromes of the empiricists and those of the dogmatics is preserved. For the syndromes which I have just discussed are characterized by evident features, whereas the ones the dogmatics talk about are not defined by evident features. In this way, empiricist reasoning, too, differs from dogmatic reasoning, in that the former concerns things evident, whereas the latter concerns things nonevident. They call their own form of reasoning "epilogism", and the form of reasoning characteristic of the dogmatics "analogism", since they do not care to agree even in their terminology. In the same way, they also call the most concise accounts not "definitions" but "descriptions". And yet nothing would prevent one from saying that an empiricist definition is the account of a thing peculiar to it, which consists solely of those features which are to be found in the thing evidently, whereas the account of the dogmatics, though it is peculiar to the thing, does not consist solely of features which are evidently manifest. As far as the terminology is concerned, it is these things, then, which are a matter of disagreement. Now, one can use words both arrogantly and humbly, as the empiricists do on many occasions, when they do not use a term in its strict sense. But the empiricists and the dogmatics also disagree with each other in matters of substance, as spelled out in the beginning, namely, in that the empiricists give credence only to those things which are evident to the senses, and to those things of which, on the basis of the former, one has some memory. The dogmatics, on the other hand, give credence not only to these things but also to those which are discovered by reason independently of observation, on the basis of the natural relationship of consequence which holds among things.

But the empiricist not only uses definitions and determinations, which rely solely on what is evident, but also makes use of causal accounts and proofs based on what has been ascertained antecedently by means of perception in an evident manner. Let us assume that, in the case of a slipped joint accompanied by a wound, a doctor is asked why he does not reset the limb. He will answer: Because it has been observed that, if something is reset under these conditions, it produces a spasm. For we have to keep in mind never to make any assertions based on logical consequence but only assertions based on evident observation and memory. It is in accordance with this, then, that the empiricist constructs his art and teaches others. And in this respect he differs greatly from the person who just pursues some irrational practice. For such a person does many things without proper determination. The empiricist equally differs from him in that he makes use of history. This we need to do because of the vastness of the art, since one man's life will not suffice to find out everything. For we accumulate these things and collect them from all sources, turning to the books of our predecessors. If those who have written about these matters had discovered each of them before they wrote about them, in such a way that an empiricist who makes use of determinations, could discover them, too, then all these things would be true, exactly as they are written down by these authors. But, since some put trust in their experience, even though it is not qualified by the proper determination, since, further, some oftentimes have not seen what they have written down, and since, moreover, some have followed rational conjectures and, as a result, have not written the truth about some matters, for all these reasons we cannot just simply believe what has been written down by our predecessors. Rather, we first have to subject it to scrutiny, before we make use of it. And this, then, is one of the features which are part of experience, but which are lacking in those who just follow some irrational practice. Menodotus calls these people "practitioners" [tribakes], making up the name himself after the word "practician" [tribon], a word in common use among ancient doctors for those who are steeped in practice in some subject. Hence one might call the person who is accomplished in the exercise of something and who has mastered the practical application of the theory a practician whereas one would call a person who applies himself to an art without the use of reason, i.e., somebody who neither knows how to make the appropriate determinations nor puts his mind to history, a practitioner. And if he does not put his mind to history, he also will not try to judge it.

Chapter VIII

on history, which is an account of what
one has perceived oneself or an account
compiled from books of those things on
which all who have written about the
matter agree

Since at this point, too, they have some short account of the name "history", let us recall the matter briefly. Some say that history is the report of those things which have been seen, but others want to add something to this, namely, the term "manifestly", and thus they say that history is a report of those things which are manifestly apparent; yet others have said that it is a report of those things which one has seen for oneself. But they all, though they give accounts which differ in wording, want these accounts to be equivalent. And hence they say of all of these accounts, in which they explain the same thing in different ways, that they are equivalent. But there are yet other accounts which actually do differ from these, in which something is added to each of the accounts which have been referred to. Let us mention one of these as an example: History is the report of those things which have been seen or of things as if they had been seen. According to this account of history, some history will be true, whereas other history will be false; according to the previous descriptions, no history would be false. Hence the critical judging of history will be a different thing, too, depending on which of the two meanings one assumes. According to the one, one will judge whether it is truly history; according to the other, whether the history is true. But we will here, too, allow everybody to call matters as he chooses to. We will discuss how one has first to judge history and then apply it in practice. To judge history is to be able to distinguish the truth and the falsity of what has been 67 written, and, furthermore, its possibility and impossibility. For this distinction, too, according to Menodotus is not without use. Since I grant that everything which is reported in books can be called "history", because the majority of doctors are accustomed to use the term this way, I ask you to heed this distinction. The first and foremost criterion of true history, the empiricists have said, is what the person who makes the judgment has perceived for himself. For, if we find one of those things written down in a book by somebody which we have perceived for ourselves, we will say that the history is true. But this criterion is of no use if we want to learn something new. For we do not need to learn from a book any of those things which we already know on the basis of our own perception. Most useful and at the same time more truly a criterion of history is agreement. For it is possible that I have never used mace (this is a drug brought from Arabia, the bark of a tree). But all who write on materia medica say about it that it constipates. Shall we, then, believe or disbelieve them? I, for my part, say that one should believe those who are in such agreement. But I say this, since we talk about matters which can be perceived. For agreements concerning what is not manifest may be very widespread; yet they are not supported by everybody who writes on the subject. And, even if one granted that it is not ruled out that such an 68 agreement could ever occur, at least the empiricist will have no share in such an agreement. But, whatever agreements come about among all men concerning matters which can be perceived, such agreements can be trusted in practical life. For, though we ourselves never have sailed around Crete or Sicily or Sardinia, we have come to believe that they are islands, because those who have perceived the matter for themselves are all in agreement with each other on this. Now, we have acquired in everyday life the experience that those who report on matters which can be perceived agree with each other. And thus we have come to believe that the stomach is constipated by mace. But in the same way it is possible that we, just on the basis of our own perception, never had any experience with reum Ponticum. Yet, turning to the books of those who have written about it, we nevertheless have come to believe that it is of use in bloodletting. Closely related to the account of history just given is another one (which is not epilogistical though, but analogistical and dogmatic) which somebody may be willing to consider who thinks that it is appropriate to trust agreement and be willing to accept that the matter itself may give an indication of its trustworthiness. For there are some who talk this way, not just among the dogmatics but also among those who call themselves empiricists because an agreement which is free from doubt is a sign of the truth of the matter. But somebody who just relies

69   on epilogism, i.e., on reasoning entirely concerned with what is manifest, cannot just talk this way but has to say that it is a matter of experience of all those who agree with each other on all matters which are evidently true. If, then, somebody were to say, on the basis of observation, that agreement is a sign of truth, he would be making an empirical judgment. If, on the other hand, one were to say this, giving the nature of the matter as one's reason, one would be making a rational judgment. One criterion for true history, then, is this, but another one is the learning and the character of the writer. Of these we have to have some experience through other writings, as in the case of Hippocrates and Andreas; the former, as an example of the greatest expertise and the highest regard for the truth, the latter, as an example of an arrogant man and somebody who in his experience falls far behind the knowledge of Hippocrates. Another criterion for history is whether what is said resembles those things we have come to know through our own observation, as in the case of mace and reum Ponticum. For both constipate, just like all other things which bring the flows of the stomach to a halt and which prevent an excessive eduction of blood.

CHAPTER IX

on transition to the similar, in which he
explains in which way one has to take
and to understand "similar" here, since
"similar" is used in many ways

Menodotus claims that transition to the similar is not a true criterion but
70   only a criterion of what is possible, at least if one assumes that practice, i.e., learning, is the true criterion. But on this matter we will have some-

thing to say a bit later. One has to take note of the fact that the transition to the similar, which by itself is a way towards experience and which is a criterion of what is possible in history, is twofold, just like the judging of history. Logical transition arrives at knowledge based on the nature of the thing in question by means of indication. Empirical transition, on the other hand, relies on what is known naturally, not because it is plausible that something similar should have similar effects, lack similar things, or be similarly affected; it is not because of this or because of anything else of this sort that one insists on transition, but only because we know from experience that similar things are like this. For it is not only in the case of similar parts of the body that experience has taught us that, if there is the same affection, the same remedies are in place, e.g., in the case of the thigh, the elbow, the leg, the arm, the foot, and the end of the hand. Similarly, if a similar affection befalls the same part of the body, the same remedies are needed, as in the case of diarrhea and dysentery.

If the affection is similar, one needs similar remedies, e.g., medlar and quince in the case of diarrhea. This, then, experience has taught us.   71 Moreover, it also has taught us to proceed to the contrary, if the observed remedies for a given affection are applied for a long time without effect. It is only reasonable, then, that they say that the transition to the contrary, too, is based on the similarity with what has been found out empirically. Rational transition, on the other hand, never suggests transition to the contrary. Transition to the similar, then, both when it takes place by itself, quite independently of judging history, but also when it is used to judge history leads us to practical, i.e., to learned experience, not because it is something which is certainly true but because it promises the discovery of what is possible, whereas the agreement in history among those who are trustworthy can already be trusted prior to the experience. But we do not yet give credence to the transition to the similar, as if it were true, before we have tested it by practical experience.

The different degrees of expectation and trust do not directly correspond to the degree of similarity in each of the cases mentioned. For similarity in one case amounts to more similarity than in another case. For one learns about similarity from experience not by accident and going about the matter haphazardly. For what is similar in shape and colour and softness and hardness has been least observed to produce similar effects, whereas what is similar in odour or in taste has been found usually to lead to the same result and, among these, more so in the case of what is similar in taste and even more so in the case of what is similar in   72 both respects, i.e., in odour and in colour. But if in addition shape, colour and consistency enter, too, one will see that things are similar to the highest degree and produce the same effects. And among the things them-

selves which are similar in taste, one should not judge similarity just by
some single quality, such as sharpness, astringency, bitterness, sweetness, harshness, sourness, or saltiness but should put one's mind to the
peculiar character of the taste as a whole. For both aloes and copper
flakes are astringent, but their tastes are quite different and medicinal.
Hence they also are not similar to quince, nor are they edible. Therefore
one should not make the transition from the apple and the medlar to
aloes and copper flakes, and one should not administer them in the case
of bowel pain and dysentery. But, in cases where something has to be
applied to a scarred superficial wound, one can make the transition to
whatever is astringent, even if it is medicinal. For we know from experience many such drugs which close things up. But in the case of dysentery
it is better to make the transition from what is edible to what is inedible,
and then only to those inedible things which have no other strong quality
associated with their astringency, least of all sharpness and bitterness.
For qualities of this kind have been observed to exacerbate all kinds of
wounds, both by themselves and when they are mixed with astringents.
That harshness and sourness are, as it were, differentiae of the astringent
is obvious. For the astringent quality gets intensified in what is sour,
whereas it is diluted in what is harsh. Hence, if one makes a transition
taking this into account, there is better hope that what is possible will
turn out to be true. For, if it definitely was the same disease for which
quince or some other astringent of this kind was observed to be effective,
you will in the case of the same disease make a transition to what is mod-
erately astringent, namely, to what, as I have said, the Greeks call "aus-
tere". But, if according to your experience it is rather sour things which
help against the disease, you will make a transition to what is sour. It is
clear then that the degree of expectation of a possible outcome is not the
same in all cases which are similar. It rather is the case that, to the extent
that the things to which we make the transition differ in similarity, there
is a different degree of expectation of the possible outcome.   ...   one
will know   ...   ...* if it is recommended by a trustworthy man against
diarrhea and if it seems very similar to things one knows from experience. But it is clear that this kind of case will raise the highest expectation
as to the possible outcome, and perhaps somebody will dare to trust it
even before having gained a practical experience of it. But, for what
neither is confirmed by history nor is similar, there is little expectation.
But thus it is reasonable to have a higher or a lower expectation also in
the case of the transition from one disease to a similar disease, depending
on the similarity between the diseases, an expectation which is dimin-

73

74

*The text is corrupt.

ished or increased, depending on whether it is confirmed by history or not. And, in similar fashion, with the transition from one part of the body to another, to the degree that there is the more or the less difference, to that degree there will be differences in expectation.

Chapter X

in which, on the basis of what he has said in the preceding chapter, starting with the passage which begins "hence, if one makes a transition taking this into account" right down to the end of that chapter, he adds some things which form a complement to what he has said earlier in the eighth chapter concerning history

But it is obvious from the following that the more or less also makes so much of a difference when it comes to judging history that we have to give credence to one thing as if it were already true, whereas another thing we credit only as being possible. For what has been stated by several trustworthy authors and what has been found by us to be so, though not often, but nevertheless a few times, what, moreover, is similar to what is known by experience already is no less credible than what has been found by experience. But, if it is only the case that trustworthy authors agree, but we ourselves have never observed the matter, nor is it similar to what is known, then our expectation is smaller. It is smaller still, if there are not many authors who have written this, but if there is only one who is trustworthy, and if we ourselves have seen it once or twice, but not many times.

   As an example I can tell you of a man in our part of Asia who suffered from elephantiasis. Up to a certain time, he lived with his relatives and friends. But then, when some, because of their contact with him, came to have the same disease, and when he already gave off a bad odour and was horrible to look at, they built a hut for him near the village on a hill next to a fountain. There they took the man, and daily they brought him food, enough for him to live. At the time of the rise of the Dog Star, when hunters were hunting in his vicinity, wine with a strong smell was brought to them in an earthenware jar. The person who brought it put it down near where the hunters were and then left.

75

76

When the time came to have a drink, the hunters followed their custom of pouring the wine into a mixing vessel and tempering it with an appropriate amount of water. Hence, when a young man took the jar and poured it out into the mixing vessel, a dead snake fell out. They were afraid that they might suffer from the drink, and hence they themselves just drank water. But later, when they left, they gave all of the wine, as if out of piety, to the man who suffered from elephantiasis, for they thought that it was better for him to die than to live. But he was cured by this potion in a miraculous fashion, for the tuberous part of his skin fell off like the shell of crustaceous animals. What was left behind seemed soft like crayfish and crabs when the shell which surrounds them falls off.

77

Something like this happened in a similar case in Asian Mysia not far from our city. A man suffering from elephantiasis went to avail himself of natural thermal waters, in the hope that this would be beneficial. His girl friend was a beautiful maid, who had many lovers. To her he entrusted with full confidence not just the matters of the household in general but also the matters of the cellar. But, while he was using the waters, they were staying in a house nearby, which was located in a dry place full of snakes. One of these snakes fell into a jar of wine which had been put down carelessly, and it died. The young woman, thinking that what had happened was a lucky find, brought the wine to her master. But he, just like the man in the hut, got cured from drinking it. These then are two cases of experience by chance. There is another, third one, in addition to these, which is based on my imitating these chance experiences.

78

A man who suffered from this illness was a philosopher. He had been very troubled by the illness for many years, and he rather wanted to die than to live. Since he was in this miserable state, I told him of the two cases mentioned above. He himself was an expert in bird augury, and he had a friend who was marvelously adept in this art. Having watched the birds, he was persuaded, and so was his friend, too, to imitate what had become known by experience. And, drinking wine thus prepared, he turned into a leper. Some time afterwards we cured his leprosy by the usual drugs.

In addition to these, there was a fourth man, who had acquired the art of capturing live snakes and who had the disease in its early stage. He got into contact with me to ask me to cure him as quickly as possible. I cut a vein and administered a purgative drug to remove black bile. I asked him to prepare the snakes he was hunting in a dish, the way one prepares eels. He was cured, and his disease passed away. Yet another man, who was rich and not from our parts, but from central Thracia came to Perga-

mum, moved by a dream. When the god then ordered him to take a daily
potion of the snake drug and to annoint his body externally with it, the   79
disease, within a matter of days, turned into leprosy. And this disease, in
turn, was healed by drugs the god prescribed. Encouraged by all these
experiences, I confidently began to use the snake drug copiously, in the
manner prescribed by the god. They call it "theriac antidote". Moreover,
I also used theriac salt, which by now many prepare by burning live
snakes, together with certain drugs, in a new earthenware vessel, to
which they also add snake food. I myself removed the heads and the tails
of the snakes, just as in the preparation of theriac rolls. But I do not
administer any of these things by itself and right away. Rather, as I have
said, I first apply purgatives and sometimes also phlebotomy, if the age
of the patient does not prevent this and if he is strong. In common with   80
many chronic diseases, one begins with the treatment of this disease in
spring. I have talked about these cases at some length, since there are
many things which are discovered by some accident and by its imitation.
For, just as good fortune here gave me the opportunity to make several
observations by encountering by chance one case in which somebody
was helped, in another case something else which belongs to the art is
found out.

Chapter XI

*in which, by way of addition, he treats of
the behaviour and the language which
befit an empiricist*

This, then, is the account of the art which is characteristic for empiricist
medicine. For the purposes of competent treatment, it does not need any
further addition. Yet those who have called themselves heads of the
school have made such additions. Hence I will not hesitate to cover this
subject, too, by giving an example of the kind of thing they say, so that it
is clear what gets said. Let us assume, then, that the question has been
raised, as, indeed, it does get raised, what the art of medicine aims at. I
claim that the empiricist who firmly holds to the line of his school will
answer the person who has raised this problem in the following fashion: I
try to cure whatever in a body is unnatural and to display my views by   81
my deeds. Hence, it makes no difference to me whether one speaks of
soundness, health, the acquisition of soundness, the acquisition of health,
of being healthy, of being healed, or of preserving and having under con-

trol what in the body is natural, so long as I am in a position to display my views by my deeds. But I hear not only that the sophists say what I have just said but also that they add other things, on which they disagree with each other and with which they waste their time in vain. I, on the other hand, do not care to get concerned with long-winded, empty discourse, since I am fully occupied with the exercise of the art and thus do not put my mind to this sort of thing. This is the response, I think, the empiricist ought to give. For, if he should try to adjudicate the dispute which has arisen over the aim of the art of medicine, he would have to deal with the theorems of dialectic which, as he himself says, he does not want to have anything to do with. But this, too, is a matter I have demonstrated in a whole book, in which it is shown what the end of the art of 82 medicine consists in. Even less the empiricist will look for arguments, like Serapion and Menodotus did. For one has to show one's art by what one does, rather than by one's reasoning, and to avoid dialectic, without which one cannot look for conclusive, syllogistic arguments. Such an empiricist then, will not try to construct such arguments, even if, in the matters I have spoken of, it does make a difference whether or not one knows the truth. Nor will he try to resolve those arguments which seem to demonstrate something which is in conflict with what is evident. Such arguments they call sophisms. But he will frown on them, and he will stay away from all other arguments which deal with matters which are not evident, keeping in mind that each of these sophisms has a persuasive power which is so difficult to resist that even the dialecticians do not readily solve them. The empiricist will not be a man of many words or of long speeches but will talk little and rarely, just like Pyrrho the Sceptic. Pyrrho had looked for the truth and, not finding it, was in doubt about all things nonevident, but in his daily activities he followed what is evident, whereas concerning everything else he remained in doubt. The empiricist's attitude towards medical matters is like the sceptic's attitude towards the whole of life. He does not lack in reputation, but he also is 83 not arrogant; he is unassuming and not boastful, just as Timon claims Pyrrho to have been. People will be full of admiration for his art, just as Hippocrates' contemporaries were for his, when he shows by his works how great it is, healing dislocations better than anybody else, making sure that joints which get dislocated frequently do not continue to suffer this, healing fractures, lesions, wounds, and conditions which others had not been in a position to heal, predicting what is going to happen, sometimes himself pointing out details of the present situation of the patient, even before questioning him, and similarly details of what already has happened in the past. For it was by doing all this that Hippocrates among all his contemporaries had the reputation of an Asclepius, not, by God, by constructing the argument "Through Three", like Serapion nor by writing the *Tripod* like Glaucias or books of countless words, which he then divides again into two parts in such a way that both are self-contained. This is what Menodotus did, who never refrained from insult and ribaldry against other doctors. Either he openly snarled like a dog, or he was just rude like a peasant and attacked people in his uncouth manner, calling them "smart guys", "paper lions", or "guilded" and using lots of other names of this kind for the dogmatic doctors and philosophers who preceded him. And yet Menodotus himself is not beyond rebuke in his empiricism but is to be counted among those who are dogmatic in their rashness to make claims, which you can gather from the commentaries I have written on what he has said in his treatise against Severus, but even more so from the set of writings in which he argues against Asclepiades, claiming that he knows with certainty that all of Asclepiades' views are false. And this in spite of the fact that, innumerable times, in many of his writings, he has demanded that one should approach all that is not manifest as if perhaps it is true and perhaps it is not true. But, in his refutation of Asclepiades, he believes with certainty that he has demolished what Asclepiades has said, as if there were absolutely nothing to it. But Pyrrho, whom he praises, was not like this but quiet and soft-spoken, using few words, as is fitting, unless there arises some necessity to say more. Such a necessity arose one day for a truly empiricist doctor, who was gaining himself a reputation through his deeds rather than through an abundance of words. He had promised to cure some grave disposition and thus was to perform some surgery and then to cure the person by means of drugs, as he was later to show by what he did. When, then, he was about to operate, a silly doctor came by and talked a lot of nonsense, trying to upset the decision by arguing that one should not use surgery on the man. The empiricist said only one thing to the patient and his relatives and thus overcame the sophistic reasonings. What he said was this: I leave for the moment, so that you, considering the words of this man and my deeds, which you have always seen, can put your trust in whom it pleases you. And, saying this, he left the house. So the sophist had to leave, too. The relatives of the patient sent him off to talk his nonsense elsewhere and sent again for the doctor who had shown his art by his deeds, entrusting the cure to him. For not the person who is a sophist nor indeed even Demosthenes himself, who had more experience in this than anybody else, would ever persuade people not to entrust themselves to those who have truly demonstrated their art through their deeds. And yet Serapion, this new Asclepius, has dared shamelessly to attack Hippocrates, who had contributed so much to the art. What Serapion left behind are works in which he praises himself as the first undogmatic

84

85

86

doctor, something one can only marvel about; he does not mention for a moment the other ancient doctors, from whom the art even to the present day draws profit.

The XIIth and Final Chapter

*in which he criticizes the Empiricists
because they claimed that perception and
memory were sufficient for the constitution
of all arts*

Far from saying that the resolutory account, i.e., the account which resolves the problems raised against Empiricism and the counterargumentative account, i.e., the account which in turn raises objections against the opponents (for this is how they call them), form part of medical experience, I rather object to those who have written such accounts, and especially to those who have written the kind of counterargumentative account which they also call "Against the Sects". For it is not their 87 view that one can judge the truth of the matters in question in these accounts, since they believe that evident perception and memory suffice for the constitution of all arts. But, to judge such matters, it is necessary to suppose that there is some power in us which is able to consider and to judge what is incompatible and what follows. If, then, there is no such power in us, we should not endeavour either to produce arguments ourselves or to refute those arguments which have been argued badly. But, if indeed there is some such power in our soul, as Heraclides of Tarentum and some other men who called themselves empiricists do believe, then they first of all have to receive further training in this ability. For I believe that there is some such power in man.

The Tarentine, too, knows very well that there is one, and he obviously uses it on many occasions. But, as one who has remained unexercised in this ability, he is as much worse a doctor than Hippocrates as he is better than Menodotus. Menodotus often introduces something third, 88 in addition to memory and perception; he calls this third thing epilogism; often, though, he does not posit anything in addition to memory except perception, as I have shown in my critique of his writings to Severus. But to write sophisms to refute, as he himself admits, other empiricists not only is uncivilized, it is rude in the extreme. For it is not a task of the art of empiricists to resolve sophisms, but the business of an Aristotle, or a Chrysippus, or others who have been trained in logical theory. But, if one should have to concede that there has to be both experience and an account of it, not only has Theodas done this sufficiently in his "Introduction", indeed, in places he has done it more than abundantly. But I already have said enough about this, too, in the comments which I have written against his "Introduction". And now I have written this book, in which I try to show in which way it is possible that someone who gives up on discovering all of medicine can acquire an art of medicine by experience without use of reason. But what Asclepiades has tried to argue in a sophistical manner, namely, that experience does not form a consistent whole, I have refuted in another book, which I compiled a long time ago. Of how much use it is in each art, if a reasoned account is added to what one has come to know by experience, has been discussed in the books "On Method of Healing". It also has been shown in some other work that there is one kind of reason which all men have by nature. In this work, I discussed common reason, and I tried to show that, of all the things on which we make pronouncements, some are known by perception alone, whereas others are known in virtue of the fact that some logical or rational knowledge of what follows or of what is incompatible is applied to what is known by perception. Moreover, I have tried to show that some of the knowledge of what follows is necessary knowledge, which those who by nature are insightful see clearly, whereas the rest is contingent and not necessary, and that most men err in rashly taking what is merely contingent to be necessary. It is in this way, too, that the disagreement among the dogmatics came about. If we stay out of this disagreement, we will have to concede defeat in a larger number of cases, but we will at least come to arrive at the same conclusions on some matters, as the geometers the calculators, and the arithmeticians do. But it so happens that for the very same reason the empiricist doctors, too, disagree with each other, as I have set forth in the commentaries on their disagreements.

[Here ends the book of Galen which is called "Outline of Empiricism", translated by Master Nicolaus of Reggio in Calabria in the year of the Lord 1341 in the month of May.]

On Medical Experience

On Medical Experience

Translation by Ḥunain *from Greek into*
Syriac, and translation by Ḥubaish *from*
Syriac into Arabic.
Galen says:

CHAPTER I

When I take as my standard the opinion held by the most skilful and wisest physicians and the best philosophers of the past, I say: The art of healing was originally invented and discovered by the logos* in conjunction with experience. And to-day also it can only be practised excellently and done well by one who employs both of these methods. Asclepiades the Bithynian, however, respected neither the earlier thinkers nor the truth, but allowed his boastfulness, arrogance, distorted reasoning and ignoble obstinacy to drive him to act shamefully and to rush blindly into wrongdoing, whereby he was emboldened to disparage and despise experience in the expectation that all men would admit him to have said something uttered by none before his time. When we reflect on what he despises and scorns, the conclusion is borne in upon us that these are arguments the confutation and rejection of which we need not consider, and we shall not seek to do so, far less do so in fact. For we find that he

---

Marginal numbers refer to pages in Walzer. The notes marked by asterisks are added by M.F.

* reason

49

frequently makes contradictory statements in which the one obviously opposes the other.

In my opinion, either he wishes to put all of us who contradict and oppose him to the test, and find out what we think—which would be more of a playful jest than a serious effort on his part—or else he is completely mad. For I really cannot think of any third motive which would account for his practices. He does not make statements which contradict each other only slightly, but employs such as are in startling opposition to one another. If you wish to understand what I mean, consider what you would think of anyone who speaks of experience as something utterly unreliable without the logos, and who asserts that experience does not exist at all, since there is nothing which can appear twice or thrice in the same way, to say nothing of its appearing very many times, as the Empiricists assert. Do you consider these to be contradictory statements or not? I, myself, regard these two views as being absolutely in opposition to one another. Now we find that Asclepiades frequently tries to affirm and maintain each of these opinions, and that he shows much determination in his effort to support and strengthen each one with the help of the other. With respect to Asclepiades, if his intentions are not serious when he defends these utterances of his in his book, we should nevertheless admonish him for his triviality and levity. But if he is putting forward a serious doctrine, then we must perforce confront him with questions, contradicting and opposing his assertions so as not to share his madness, even if there are some Sophists to-day who do not hold our view. I cannot understand therefore why they are serious, if Asclepiades only meant to be trivial and humorous and why, if it is his ambition and his aspiration to say extraordinary, novel, and absurd things which have induced him to do so—he is exceedingly fond of such conduct, and his attitude in these arguments against Empiricism is dictated by the same motive as led him into another argument shamelessly and heedlessly composed by him—why, I say, should they allow themselves to be led astray and to share this error, when they themselves cannot, even now, make any new and original statements? It is perhaps bad and odious enough for them to attack truth and to confuse it with one thing or another simply because they like novelty and prefer to advance something that has hitherto been non-existent. But worse than this and more reprehensible still, is that against their own wishes they consent to make mistakes similar to the mistakes of those who lived before them. Or perhaps some of them may have accepted the false teachings of their predecessors who initiated them into the notions which deceive them. If it had not been so, they would not display so much zeal in them nor cling so firmly to them. I think, however, these people deserve to be credited with belonging to the former (class of persons), since only ignorance of the real facts of the matter has led them into error.

CHAPTER II

We shall therefore begin by explaining the point at which they began to go wrong and stumble. And since this is our object in our argument, we   87
must make it an argument capable of being understood by youth, because for people of this class an exposition is difficult and obscure when its author begins to argue before bringing up the subject of blame and association. It is therefore imperative for us to start by considering the nature of the attack and the accusations which call for refutation by us.

I shall start my exposition without making use of the words with which Asclepiades begins his speech, but first of all in this connexion I shall try to make this point clear, that although I am able to choose a better and more convincing form of expression than his, I think it would be best and wisest for me to speak the truth, and I am unwilling to deceive those listening to my narration with convincing yet lying words, and to gain thereby unmerited praise. Since this is my intention, you must not allow yourself to think that what I am about to say first against Empiricism in this book is my own personal opinion, or that the second argument I use in support of Empiricism is my own view. Rather shall I let one of the Dogmatists bring forward the first argument, which is similar to Asclepiades' view, and the second argument shall be laid down by a representative of the Empiricists, Menodotos if you like, or Serapion, or Theodosius. As for the readers of my book, they must use their discernment and powers of reasoning when considering both arguments, and, after critically weighing their merits, see which of the two is more correct. For the reader who has attentively and eagerly exercised his mind in this book will the more easily and readily comprehend what I have dealt with in my book on the ariste hairesis.*

* best sect

CHAPTER III

And now let the Dogmatist speak first, as if he were before the judge in a court of law, ridiculing the arguments of the Empiricist, his opponent, in the following manner. Would the Empiricists affirm the primitive doctrine of the third medical school, that is to say those who call themselves aspirants of the 'technical' method (*i.e. methodikoi**), in agreeing with them that it is not necessary to reflect upon or inquire into lands, seasons, ages of man, natures, customs, salient causes, and similar things, and would they limit themselves to retaining in their memories what they have learned of diseases by observation, and be content with this method alone? If so, they might perhaps be able to assert that something appears to them as observers in the same manner very many times. Since, however, they have already acquired so much understanding and intelligence as to know that it is impossible to gain anything useful by experience without ascertaining and observing all such things, I should like to know the reason for the disparagement which has led them to neglect the logos and base all their views on experience with which no logos is connected, and place confidence in it alone. Do you think that they do not know that in the almost endless variety of their diseases and the symptoms of them the sick themselves differ from one another as well as in the above-mentioned respects—seasons of the year, lands, and similar things? Or is it that their hearts are blind and their minds too dull to understand this? Or is this something which they know full well, but desire to comprehend that which is infinite by bringing it into the category of temporal experience without making use of the logos? Should they really wish this, then let them know that the sounds of speech, though endless in number, could not be retained and comprehended by mere memory, but that a wise man grasped them and limited them, because, having reflected upon them and examined them, he discovered that the principles and the elements of which these sounds are composed—I mean the letters—are twenty-four in number according to Greek reckoning. So also with respect to triangles. For he who brought them out of infinity was not one of those who make use of Empiricism without the logos, but here too it was discovered by means of the logos that the sides of the triangle are three kinds in all, that is to say, that the triangle has either three equal sides, or that two sides are equal, or that all the sides are unequal, and that the angles of the triangle are of three kinds, I mean the right angle, the acute angle, and the obtuse angle. There is not one amongst the endless number of triangular shapes that does not fit into this scheme. So

88

89

* Methodists

also with the kinds and varieties of musical sounds: they, too, are very numerous in loudness and softness, strength and lightness, and memory cannot hold them all and confine them without the logos, but rather the logos alone, which musicians make use of, encloses and confines them, bringing them within finite categories. Is it your opinion, then, that only in the subject with which physicians are concerned the memory has simply to deal with simple and isolated things, and that there are no combinations and varieties in it?

Chapter IV

If, however, you affirm this, we would say: what is more manifold, more complicated, and more varied than disease? Or how does one discover that a disease is the same as another disease in all its characteristics? Is it by the number of the symptoms or by their strength and power? For if a thing be itself, then, in my opinion, it must be itself in all these characteristics, for if even one of them is lacking it is perverted and ceases to be itself, since it no longer possesses the quality lacking. We shall, however, concede them this point and allow that this disease which showed itself just now is, in all its characteristics, the same disease as before. In granting them this also, however, it can perhaps occur that this (disease) proves to be identical with the other two or three times but not very many times. Moreover, if it could happen very many times, no single individual could ever see it. Should he who sees it at this moment be other than the one who saw it at a different time, there is nothing to show that it was seen very many times; for the observer, and he who retains in his memory what was observed and remembered, must continually, perpetually, and uninterruptedly observe it. Again, what is regarded and observed must of necessity be observed by many people, since the case is as I have described it. How can a person determine whether what he sees at this moment is identical with that which someone else has seen before or is something quite different, unless he himself has seen both? Now, lest they imagine that in pursuing our scrutiny and argument to these lengths we are injuring them and desirous of contending with them, we would for our part make also this concession and allow that it is indeed possible that a certain disease with all its symptoms is identical with another disease, and that one individual sees it very many times.

90

CHAPTER V

Further we must reflect at this point whether this is in any way advantageous to them; for my part, I think it is of no advantage to them at all. For if one were to be satisfied with mere observation of the number of symptoms by themselves without requiring to consider also their order, and which is first and second and third, some advantage might probably be derived therefrom. Now, however, it is found that by changing the order of some of the symptoms and by removing them from their places, or acting similarly in the case of some diseases, this disease is not only different from the foregoing one, but is frequently its reverse, because the similarity and consistency are void and perverted. What I am now going to explain to you shows best of all the correctness of our opinion: if, for example, convulsion follows fever, this is a sign of death, and if fever follows convulsion this is a sign of safety. So, too, when lethargy precedes trembling, it is not a sign of death, but if it follows trembling it is a very bad sign. Further, in regard to 'sour intestines' (oxyregmia), if this occurs after the disease known as 'slippery intestines' (leienteria) it is a good sign, but not if the reverse is the case. We know also that when a man is overtaken by the disease described as 'loss of memory', and on getting rid of it is immediately attacked by the disease known as 'phrenitis', this is better than if the man suffering from 'phrenitis' were afterwards to be attacked by 'loss of memory'. Again, if anyone requires a bandage and his intestines are full of the waste products of digestion, and one administers an enema first, and then bandages him, this is a great help to him, but if one treats him in the reverse order, no little harm can be done to him. In my opinion, too, the taking of nourishment after the application of ointment and bandages is frequently useful, but it is not good to apply ointment, to bandage, or to undertake any other manipulation after the patient has taken nourishment. It is not surprising that such changes in order and sequence among the sick are of great potency, since we find that bathing and gymnastic exercises immediately after meals are bad for healthy persons, but if they do the reverse and partake of food after these exercises, they derive great benefit therefrom. This is a fact, although there is a vast difference between a healthy person and a sick one, for the sick remain a shorter time in the same state and change more rapidly from one condition to the other, and are altogether more open to danger than are those who enjoy health. This, indeed, is so perfectly obvious that it hardly calls for argument. If then with a healthy person, who is nearly always more or less in the same condition, one cannot conjoin the things in which he is engaged absolutely and at haphazard, how much less possible is it to do so in the case of the sick? We ought not to strive

91

54

after such foolishness. But I shall not desist even at this point, nor hold my peace. On the contrary, I shall concede this to them also and admit the veracity of those things which resemble the delusions of a madman, and are in very truth dreams and visions.

CHAPTER VI

But now consider further, if this is in any way useful to them, or if they have not lost the whole of that which they are striving for. If anyone were to concede all these things, numerous as they are, and should grant them all—and I should support them, if they conceded these things in friendly argument—they would (still) be as far from acquiring the knowledge they desire as I am from flying. For with respect to the salient causes of diseases they are exposed to greater doubt than in what was mentioned before. For someone may say: tell me, why is it that lassitude, burning caused by the sun, drunkenness, overeating, exposure to a cold atmosphere, overstepping the limits with regard to coition, and indigestion are things which must be remembered and inquired into, and to which reason must be applied, but other things, analogous to these, need not be made the subject of investigation? I mean by analogous things inquiring as to whether the sick man took a bath before the onset of his illness or not; whether he had lived in the town or in a village; whether he had stayed in a room or on a terrace and if he had slept or had lain awake, or if he had been depressed or had had worries, or if he had read some book. More remote from this would be the query as to whether he had worn a white garment before that time, or a red, or a black, or a crimson one. Furthermore, one might ask whether he had wrestled or had bathed with anyone, dined or slept with anyone. For all this and similar things, although there are others more remote than these, they must retain in their memories and investigate, when they have even once refused to disown the memorizing of what they see of the salient causes.

92

For if they would, like us, investigate these things, by way of determining the causes of diseases, they would very easily be able to distinguish and differentiate between them and the things which are not the causes of disease. Since, however, according to their own statement, they do not investigate these things by way of determining the causes of diseases, but as parts of the symptoms in their totality, how can they say that there are things which must be investigated and memorized as being single symptoms of the totality of symptoms, and other things which are not so? And it is just this very doubt and this very question to which they are exposed and constrained in regard to the remedies for diseases. For here, too, they are unable to differentiate between that which is ineffectual and harmful, and that which is useful and beneficial. For in the case of one particular sick person many things are found together: things which his body has assimilated and things which are evacuated, also things which externally affect the body. Since all this can have but one result, either improvement in the condition of the sick man or a turn for the worse, the Empiricists are quite unable to assure themselves as to which of these things must be made the cause of the sick man deriving benefit, when he is benefited, and which of them must be regarded as the cause of his being harmed, when he has been harmed. For because they only retain in their memories what comes at the end of the case, they can only have the knowledge that this has occurred very many times after such things have taken place. But that certain things are the cause of a sick man's recovery or death, and others are not, is a matter of which they are quite ignorant. This conclusion is borne in upon us in the most trivial and unimportant cases. Suppose that a man is attacked by cataract and he is loosened, and his eye is anointed, and he goes for a walk and reads, and his condition afterwards becomes worse, or if you prefer it improves, would the Empiricist be able to know which of these things was harmful and which was useful, if he did not observe the nature of each single one of them? What advantage has observation to him who knows nothing of this? But just because the number of concomitants of diseases is so great and there is such variety in what causes evacuation and what is vomited up and what is introduced into the organism, while those things that affect it from outside are still more numerous, the Empiricist is still less able to judge which of them are beneficial and which harmful. Let me say something which, in my opinion, is straightforward and most correct: I am sure that anyone who does not investigate things at the very outset and reflect upon them carefully is not capable at some later date even of beginning to memorize them, not to speak of anything more. And how can anyone do this who does not know from the very beginning what things have to be eliminated and disregarded as being superfluous and unnecessary, and what things have to be examined and to be judged carefully as to their usefulness and their necessity. However, on account of the Empiricists' negligence, which has overstepped all limit, I shall make a concession to them even here.

Chapter VII*

For, even if we grant them all this, the Empiricists still need many further concessions to arrive at the conclusion they want to arrive at. For, if I should not be able to show that the absurdities which remain are as serious as the ones already mentioned, I would think of myself as of no good even for them. Now I know very well that you have been wondering, by God not about us, but about the simplemindedness of the Empiricists, who accept all these concessions which touch on such grave matters, and yet are no better off for it; a new set of fallacies, no less grave, just takes the place of the previous ones. They show complete ignorance, an abundance of shamelessness, and an insensitivity which almost goes beyond that of matter, when they do not know where to start from, and when, even when one grants them that one can see a thing happen in the same way very many times, they still are in no position to see, or to remember, or to write down, such myriads of differences as one finds in patients. Which library would have place for so large a history, which soul could store the memory of so many things? And nevertheless, they even thus do not realize that we concede them all this, as if it were in jest; instead they treat it as something certainly true and even pride themselves in what they go on to say as a result. Now I will show clearly, not for their sake, for there is no point in arguing with stones, but in order to bring the argument to a conclusion, that even if it be conceded that something can be seen to happen in the same way very often, they nevertheless will not be able to produce a technical theorem on the basis of this. And so that nobody should think that I am just availing myself of an argument of Plato's, namely the argument that if some special occupation manages to provide a grasp of the nature of the subject-matter it concerns itself with, then it is an art, but if not, it is just some practice and mere experience, but not an art ("For I do not, he says, call anything an art which is just an unreasoned pursuit."); I do not use this argument, not because it is not true. I would be out of my mind, if I said that. It is rather that the Empiricists, in their lack of shame, readily admit this, too; they will say that they do not care whether, because of this, one does not call their occupation an art, but something else. Which arguments, then, do I have to offer? The first one is an argument whose premises are conceded even by them. For I take it that it is the observation of things which have been seen to happen in the same way very many times which they call experi-

*This part of the text down to p. 59, line 7 is extant in Greek; Walzer here printed the Greek text instead of an English translation from the Arabic; this section has been translated by M.F.

ence. Thus it is composed of many things each of which has been seen once. But they themselves also say that what has been seen just once does not amount to something technical. Hence, what has been observed very many times is composed of many things each of which is non-technical. The argument could also be presented in the following way. If what has been observed once is non-technical, but what has been observed very many times is composed of many things which have been observed once, then what has been observed very many times is non-technical. But what has been observed once is, indeed, non-technical. Hence, the same is true of what has been observed very many times. But perhaps they will claim that they do not understand what we are saying. For they will confess that they shun logic just as all the other sciences. With your permission, let us then leave this argument which we have constructed ourselves aside, and, instead, direct another argument against them which runs like this: can you tell us, Empiricists, how many times very many times is? For we ourselves desire to gain knowledge through observation the way you do. Hence, to make sure that we do not, for a lack of measure, miss the appropriate amount, either because we think that we already have come to the end before we have observed the matter sufficiently, or because, out of our ignorance of the proper measure, we extend our observation far beyond what is appropriate, we ask you to show us, too, what the measure is, so that we, too, can learn something from observation. "You silly fool, he replies laughing, you ask for the unit. There is no single measure for all things, but it is a different one for each case. To raise the question you have asked is like asking the shoemaker to teach one which last it is he fits all shoes on. For in that case, too, there is no single measure for all feet, because they are unequal. Nor is there in this case a single measure for all things, since they differ." I am pleased, accept this answer, and indeed am glad that he did not promise to tell me one measure for all things. For I would have had my doubts, in case he had announced that he would introduce one measure derived from things which differ a lot from each other. But as it is, if he only were to show me some specific measure for each kind of thing, I would have great hope to grasp the truth. Beginning, then, with simpler matters I ask how often I have to see a lesion of the dura mater before I know exactly whether the patient will die, either always, or for the most part, or rarely, or half of the time. But not one of them has given us in our days an answer as to the measure, nor has anyone written it down in his books. Does this not suggest that they do not have a definite answer for the particular case, either? It is clear to everybody that their case by now has collapsed. What is left is to continue to banter in the manner in which we have argued with them right from the beginning, and thus to even now consider, to preserve good manners, whether they just do not know what the measure for what has been seen very many times is, though in the nature of things there is such a measure, or whether it is altogether impossible that it should turn out that there is some measure by means of which we judge what is to count as very many times and which would have the effect that what previously was not technical now is technical. I have considered the matter often.

I should not otherwise venture to decide such important matters off-hand, but I am now going to tell you how, after due reflection and investigation, it has become plain to me that there is no standard by which a thing may be judged as having been seen very many times. Now, reflect upon my words and consider them carefully, and see if I am in error, or if I correctly apply the principles on which the structure of proof rests, whether of the opinion I hold and of which I am convinced, or of the things which they support and hold to be convincing. For they say that a thing seen but once cannot be accepted nor regarded as true, neither what was seen a few times only. They believe something can only be accepted and considered true, if it has been seen very many times, and in the same manner every time. I would ask them, therefore, if that which has been observed ten times is included in that which has been seen very many times, and their answer to this is 'No'. Then I would say to them: 'And what has been seen eleven times?'—and they say 'No'. Then I would ask them further about a thing that has been seen twelve times—and they say 'No'. Again, I would ask: 'And what has been seen thirteen times?', and they say: 'Neither has this reached the required limit'. And so I never cease asking and adding another number to each until I reach a high number. Nothing remains for him thus questioned except either to deny at a given time that the number has reached the limit when one can say it constitutes very many times, or, should he admit that it has, to make himself a laughing-stock for men, since he would thus require them to allow him a number reached solely by a usage fixed by himself, and a decision made by him alone. For one might say to him: Why, for example, should anything that was seen fifty times be regarded as having been seen very many times, and that which was seen forty-nine times is not regarded as having been seen very many times. In affirming this, you place yourself in the position of one who affirms two mutually contradicting things. You have previously acknowledged that what was seen once is not to be accepted and does not belong to that which may be considered true. But here now we see you admit that it is acceptable and is to be considered true. For if something that was seen forty-nine times and yet in all these times was not accepted nor considered to be true, now by the addition of this one single time comes to be considered acceptable

96

97

and true, it is obvious that only by being seen a single time has it become acceptable and true. The inevitable conclusion is that seeing a thing once—although at the outset this was not accepted and considered true— has on this occasion such force that when added to something which was not acceptable and not considered true as to make it acceptable, and vice versa.

CHAPTER VIII

These then are the arguments used by the Dogmatists against the Empiricists with respect to the question of 'seeing-very-many-times'; and they are arguments to be stored in one's mind and recalled to memory. As for the other arguments, one hardly knows what to say about them, for they are exceedingly bad and absurd, and are one and all potentially to be classed in this category of arguments. For if you were to inquire what weapons the Empiricists use, you would find that they employ two methods of argument and speech: the one is short and concise, the other more detailed, their manner being to refute by the method of contradiction every single point which we have mentioned. And each of their arguments remind the opponent of things of a kind which the Dogmatists have to acknowledge to the Empiricists are plain and lucid.

Now all the refutations brought by the Dogmatists against the Empiricists may be collected into three groups. For some there are who declare that by the 'seeing-very-many-times' of a thing nothing can be ascertained, and that all discoveries are made by the logos alone. Others admit that of the simple, isolated things which in the case of simple symptoms cleave to one's memory, one after the other may be discovered by 'seeing-very-many-times'. But with respect to the other things they reject such as a method of discovery, and will have nothing to do with it. And the remaining third group is of opinion that even if one were to admit that by 'seeing-very-many-times' such things could be ascertained, yet the discovery of everything by experience without logos is impossible, and this, in my opinion, because of the number of diseases and their accompanying symptoms which in themselves are endless owing to the isolation of each case. And we understand by endlessness the variations in their degree and arrangement which complicate the diseases and their symptoms through some of them preceding and some following others.

CHAPTER IX

And the type of argument by which the first group of these three is characterized, is one which opposes the whole of the arts (technai) in general and, furthermore, rejects what is obvious to the eye, and contradicts all habits and customs of life adopted by mankind. And it also opposes him who speaks and him who argues with it. For they (the Empiricists) say: 'O you who reject experiences because they neglect inquiry into the nature of things, what think you of the nautes*—i.e. he who steers a ship upon the ocean? Is he, until he has fathomed the logos of nature and discovered the elements of the whole, and examined the nature of the winds, unable to sail forward at a given moment, and to be aware of things before they happen—to know (e.g.) of the storm that is coming up on him, and can he not steer his ship after this has taken place until he reaches the place whither he wished to sail? And what think you, moreover, of the peasant? Is he, until he has learned from one of the philosophers something of the nature and substance of the soil, and what is the nature and substance of rain and wind, and how they come about, unable to know by experience what seeds to sow at certain times and on what soil, if they are to spring and flourish and attain completion and perfection? And what think you of the vine-grower? Must he, too, examine the nature of the vineyard? And do you think that the consumer of foods needs to draw inferences and to inquire into their nature and substance, and is not content to know of each one of them its action and effect upon the body (by experiencing) many times what results from it? And the agreement of mankind that at the time of the rising of the Pleiades harvest must start, and at the time of their setting ploughing should begin— do you hold that it is not sufficient to learn this by experience, but that this must be closely observed and attentively examined until the nature of the constellation of the Pleiades, and the nature of the Bear, of Sirius, and that of the other stars has been studied? And tell me, what about the shoemaker? Can he not know before ascertaining the nature of cattle and the nature of sheep, which skins are stronger, which more flexible? Is this not all absurd and ponderous and like the pastime of Sophists who abandon themselves to trivialities and idle talk? You know that men taken as a whole, of whatever type they may be, do not feel bound to examine into the nature of wine, but that they know perfectly well that too great indulgence in drinking wine is harmful. And so it is with mushrooms. One finds that the learned man who discourses on the natures of things, knows their nature. But if any mushrooms are placed before him, he

99

* pilot

61

does not know which are edible and which are not, whereas the country-dwellers can distinguish between them since they are familiar with them and see them constantly, and even the children know them, to say nothing of their elders. And likewise one finds that the baker knows which kind of wheat makes unadulterated bread and which does not, whereas you, O learned investigator of the nature of seeds, are ignorant in this respect. And in short, we find that of the bulk of mankind each individual by making use of his frequent observations gains knowledge not attained by another; for as Demokritos says, experience and vicissitudes have taught men this, and it is from their wealth of experience that men have learned to perform the things they do. Now since this is the case, what do you think about it? Is it logical to admit that in all other experiences, although the nature of the thing utilized is unknown, that is achieved which ought to be achieved, and to wrong medicine alone denying this to it—or do you say that the things which are known by other kinds of experience are stored up in the minds of those inhabitants of prosperous cities, who are possessed of insight and understanding, and those who in their nature are of a higher degree than the other people in these cities, but the things which are ascertained by medical experience, since they are inferior and lower, can only be memorized by simple-minded people like one Mammakythos or Meletides or others of those famed and known for their simplicity? But you know that this cannot be maintained, for I think that you too, who attack the method of experience, are agreed with us, that medicine is a thing which has passionately interested the best and most excellent of men. And the only difference between us is that you assert that these people did not deduce what they have deduced from experience, but by inferring what is concealed from what is manifest.

100

CHAPTER X

And again, I assert that what you have been striving to prove by your arguments is exceedingly bad and absurd. You reject, namely, the empirical because it aims to store up particular things, and for other reasons you praise and value the method of inference from the visible to the invisible, because in this way one learns in a general and comprehensive manner what one wishes to know. For instance, in the case of anyone wishing to treat a patient suffering from diarrhoea, it would be more useful and helpful to know that preparations conducive to constipation would benefit him than to know that quinces or pomegranates would benefit him. For knowledge of general things embraces both of these, and with them very many others, and comprises almost everything beneficial to the sufferer from diarrhoea. But the Empiricist, were he to mention and enumerate fifteen varieties of what would be helpful—to say nothing of his enumerating and mentioning only three or so—would not even then have come to an end of them, because those he has not mentioned are even more. And moreover, if one were to grant them that they were able to mention in their books everything that physicians could make use of for purposes of healing—although this is impossible—no one could remember all these things without having some generalization on which to rely, and without all these things being united by some single thing in which they are all alike. According to their argument, the characteristic of the logos is that everything it elucidates, it elucidates at once, and the characteristic of empiricism, that it elucidates little by little, gradually. And it is for them to tell us whether Hippocrates in his day—since they assert that the whole of medical knowledge was elucidated simultaneously—had at the very outset commanded the whole of medical science. Should they say that this is the case, then it must necessarily follow that Hippocrates' effort in setting down in his book *Epidemics* what he desired to be a memorial to his observation and memorizing was a vain and useless one. Or would they say that Hippocrates discovered much, and that those who followed after have not discovered less, and that one finds up to the present day that some things have already been discovered, and other things it is hoped to discover later. Should they say this, then the gradual discovery of a thing is more proper and more congenial to the empirical method than to the logos. And should this be the case—we believe, however, that it is not so—then not only is the view of those wrong who declare that nothing can be discovered by experience, but the view of those who say that everything is discovered by experience is certainly true. And beside the other points which the logic of the arguments forces upon the Dogmatists, there further follows of necessity for them that inquiry into the origins of medicine is a vain and superfluous thing. For you Dogmatists say that inquiry into that matter is only useful in so far as it was needed to discover what had not yet been discovered in the past, so that you can apply it, and by this means discover what you wish to discover.

But if everything is discovered by the logos, then it is no longer necessary for us to discover anything supplementary to what has already been found, and inquiry into how something that is used in medicine was discovered is useless and vain. And further the facts that you acknowledge and agree with us that up to the present much has not been discovered beyond what has already been discovered, and also that in the existing

101

102

things we are forced to make a transference from one thing to another of a similar nature, prove clearly even to the unintelligent—to say nothing of the others—that matters concerning medicine are not to be discovered by the logos. And I do not know how it has happened that this argument about methods has led clearly to the possibility that by the logos which consists in inference from the visible to the invisible nothing has been discovered, although this was not our purpose or intention, but we desired rather to show that not everything can be discovered by this logos. And there are other arguments, too, besides this one, which conform to this aim and tend in the same direction. For if nothing is discovered by means of the logos in conjunction with experience, then one 'who knows the natures' can do everything without the aid of experience, and achieve a healing of the body by means of that whereto the logos alone leads and directs him, which is not inferior to the healing of one who possesses a knowledge of both these things. And one who bases his method of healing only on that whereto experience alone leads him, cannot possibly know anything technically or accomplish anything that is technical. But this is not the case; on the contrary, if 'those who know the natures' were familiar with the discussion, argument, and logos in matters concerning medicine but lacked the knowledge gained by experience, they would never carry out any operation of medicine well, however small and trivial. And as for those who in the practice of medicine follow that whereto simple experience alone leads them, we frequently find very many of them who in the practice of medicine have attained a high measure of excellence. And from this it is seen that experience by no means requires the logos, and that the logos is of no use in the art of medicine. But too much time has been spent in speaking and arguing of this theme, and it has prepared the way for part of what we need for what we propose to go on to prove.

103   CHAPTER XI

For it is obvious from it that not only *can* some part of what is discovered be discovered by experience, but that experience by itself suffices for what we require without our having any need of the logos, and along with these two things it is also obvious that by drawing conclusions from the visible to the invisible the logos either alone or in conjunction with experience can achieve nothing useful. And it is my opinion that the views and arguments which we intend to set forth will make just this very thing clear. For we have a question to put to them which we are justified and right in asking. And the question is: Why do physicians who make use of the method of deduction from the visible to the invisible differ not a little but very much amongst themselves, although they are very numerous, in the views by which each one of them claims to have knowledge of things instrumental in healing, but agree in the diagnosis, treatment, and healing of diseases? Do you not think it is astonishing, seeing that these people are so numerous, to find that they are of different opinions on a given matter, such as digestion and assimilation, and that to such an extent that one of them asserts that there is no such thing in this world as digestion, and another declares that digestion and assimilation exist indeed, but resemble the process of cooking, and another says they do not resemble cooking at all, but rather decay —for this is what a man named Pleistonikos(?) has said—and another follows these two, and imagines, just as men imagine things in dreams, that assimilation and digestion consist in the dissolving of food into a juice like the drink made from barley (ptisane), and another is of opinion that the food is ground and pounded, and another says that it is the work of the pneuma caused by a peculiarity contained therein? And you will find that Erasistratos has confused and mixed up many things, for he attributed a part of the process of assimilation and digestion to warmth and the greater part to grinding and pounding, and has set forth in many passages his belief that this takes place only through the connexion of the food with the pneuma. And when one sees that the absurdity of these people goes so far in regard to one universally recognized fact of nature, and then that when they visit the sick they put aside their foolishness and all admit that this 104 kind of food perishes quickly, that another is slow to perish, that this is easily digested, and another indigestible, what do you think he will do? Will he ask them anything else but the question: How is it that you are of the same opinion and are unanimous with respect to the easily digested and the indigestible kinds or food? And he will say: I think, or rather I do not doubt, that you were unanimous in this matter, because you were guided by one thing (which you all accept); but the logos is not uniform, universal, comprising all of you, because you have different views and each one of you holds an opinion completely contradictory to the opinion of the others. And since this is the case, then nothing remains except experience, and since nothing but this remains, it is obvious that you practise medicine by the method of experience alone.

CHAPTER XII

This position has been countered by someone (Alexandros, I think, or one of his disciples) with an argument which owing to his lack of education and his ignorance is absurd. His contention is that it is not impossible by means of various logoi to discover one and the same thing. And we call upon Allah for aid against this extraordinary and strange effort of this endless absurdity and folly. If he whose opinion is correct in every matter is not to be ranked above him who has no correct view in any matter but is wrong in everything, then what ails you that you argue with one another and refute one another, and why do you boast of having discovered truth and its substance when he whose opinion is correct is not ranked above him whose view are wrong in the application of the logos? But I do not think that I need enter into a long argument to prove that they can discover things by experience alone, and that it is impossible for anything to be discovered except by experience. For this is a matter which one can easily take from them (i.e. the Dogmatists).

But whoever of them denies this must think that Hierocles said something worthless when he maintained that the logos which consists in the conclusion from the visible to the invisible uses the facts of experience and sets them up as premises. We, however, find that this view is not worthless, and that this matter cannot be otherwise than as Hierocles says, since the Dogmatists, when they investigated each of the natural functions, made use of experience at the very outset. When, for example, they inquire into assimilation and digestion, you may hear one of them asserting that heat is one of the causes, and with this assumption he begins his exposition. He says: Since the most effectual aids to digestion are those of the teeth(?) which contain most heat, and those seasons of the year which store the maximum amount of bodily heat in the stomach, and those crafts and activities which heat the body most, and of the influences which affect the body from without those which produce heat, one must conclude that digestion in the body is caused solely by heat. And listen how the exponent of this view produces many instances of this in order to support his argument that the digestion of each kind of food resembles the process of cooking. He says namely, that the rockfish is easily digested, his proof for this statement being that it is quickly cooked, while, on the other hand, beef is not easily digested, the proof of this being that it becomes fit to eat only after much labour in cooking. But we say to the exponent of this view: O you wise man, whence do you know this of which you speak, in order that you can understand by it something of the function of digestion? For surely, after having seen each of these things but once, you will not say that you dare to erect the struc-

105

66

ture of your argument on what you have seen but once, but you would blush to say so and disgrace yourself by using an untrue argument. For it is quite possible that at the outset you might meet with someone who can digest beef more easily and quickly than rock-fish. If you believe and accept as correct what you have seen in this person, and then begin to inquire why beef is more quickly and easily digested than rock-fish, you will most certainly fall into a mistake from the very outset, since the thing, the cause of which you investigate, is in itself not true. And as this is the case, it is indeed necessary that you do not take for granted what you observe at first, and do not believe that what you see once is always the case; and he who has seen such a thing must wait until he has seen it a second time. When he sees it a second time, than the second case must either resemble the first—as this is not impossible—or differ from it, the rock-fish having been more easily digested than the beef. Whatever the case may be, I believe myself that you must wait until you see this a third time. For if the second was the opposite of the first, what can you make of two contradictory things, and what conclusion can you arrive at in your mind from these two things, and how dare you give precedence to the first rather than to the second, or to the second rather than to the first, after having seen each of them only once? And if you have observed the thing twice in the same way, then we still say that you should wait until you see it a third time. If, however, you prefer to consider what you have already seen to be correct, then do so. I, personally, do not covet, envy, or grudge you your conclusion. Yet consider what will perchance befall you if you believe this to be correct, namely, that you will imagine beef to be more digestible than rock-fish—a belief that is not in accordance with truth. Since this is so, you must of necessity wait in order to see the third case, yet even this you will not find capable of creating as strong a belief that knowledge of the nature of the matter in question becomes certainty in consequence. And this rests on just those very doubts which you may consider trivial and neglect. For I have observed that you often use the method of neglecting and leaving aside things which present themselves to you, and which you cannot refute, and about which there is some doubt, as if they were things you could not accept, but must rather reject because of their absurdity. Moreover, after observing a third case, you must either think you have learnt something and have grasped some chapter in medical science, or else, if you do not think this after having seen the third case, you will most certainly do so, after you have observed four of five cases. And this is something which, apart from being obviously wrong, is opposed to your own view. For one has the right to ask you why a thing which has been seen five times becomes acceptable and unassailable in your view, while one seen four times only

106

has not yet attained to this degree. But that is an argument introduced only by the way, and with no particular aim in view.

107   The argument which we were maintaining is this, that the Dogmatists base their arguments upon certain premises, and then assert that these premises point to other things outside of themselves. For example, the Dogmatist praises certain teeth, those namely which are chiefly instrumental in furthering digestion; he praises them because of the power of the digestive organs, not because of the quantity of heat. And he likewise praises winter as being of all the seasons the one most conducive to digestion. Likewise he asserts that the crafts and occupations which are most conducive to a good digestion are those which strengthen the body. Again, one of them will say that foods which are easily and quickly ground and pounded are the easiest and quickest of digestion, and the foods that are the reverse of this are difficult of digestion. And in my opinion you would find, were you to consider this carefully, that Erasistratos, the most decided exponent of this view, in the premises which he puts forward in answer to the objections brought against his views, does not build up his case on the logos and on conclusion from the visible to the invisible, but on experience. He says, for example: We can discern many violent things which suddenly affect the body without in any way harming the (bodily) heat, and yet we find that in these circumstances we do not digest as well as we digested previously. So this man, as we see, directs his criticism against those who would make heat the cause of digestion, but it does not escape our notice that in this he obtains his premises from experience. But the punishment which he has justly merited has overtaken him also. For Asclepiades likewise selects his premises from experience and says: We see that many kinds of food are easily ground and pounded, notwithstanding which they are difficult to digest, and herein is a proof that digestion does not take place through food being ground and pounded.

CHAPTER XIII

And since matters are as you have seen with respect to these two men, the conclusion according to the claims of the one is in contradiction with that claimed by the other. We find, namely, that they seek to investigate, as they assert, the causes of the things which are found by observation, and to differentiate between their truth and falsity, so that they may recognize the natures of these causes. Moreover we find that they base their arguments in this on things known by experience, and that they make
108

use of these in positing what they wish to posit and validate, and in the rejection of what they do not want. And you can recognize these people by their absurd and distorted views and (conclude that) what is left after subtracting their arguments is the truth. Following up this point I maintain that there is no one who disputes or denies the fact that vinegar aids digestion. But with respect to the question in what way and by what power it is enabled to do so, we find none who are agreed. For one says: Vinegar easily and quickly dissolves everything with which it is mixed by breaking it up into small parts, and so it is with the process of digestion. And another is of opinion that it is not for this reason that vinegar is so helpful to digestion, but rather because it is warm. And these two differ simply because the first one imagines, just as a sleeper imagines things, that in the process of digestion the stomach grinds and pounds the food, and the second supposes that it is caused by the stomach cooking the food. Another then comes to you, and upbraids this dreamer saying: What do you mean, O ignorant man? Dare you say that vinegar is warm, when it is actually exceptionally cold? And since the case of the Dogmatists is as I have described, we contradict them and say: O you wise men, if you all agree that vinegar aids digestion but, on the other hand, are not unanimous as to the manner of its efficacy, who amongst all those who have understanding, think you, would spin theories about the reason for which it is efficacious, when he can ascertain without knowing the cause thereof what foods are quickly digested? How dare you say then that these things are found and discovered by investigating the natural functions, and reject the view that these are things we have known by experience from the very outset, and that the logos has no place here, and is moreover incapable of eliciting anything, except contradiction and opposition in argument in a convincing manner?

As for me, I am surprised at the Sophists of our age, who are unwilling   109
to listen to the word of Hippocrates when he says: 'in the case of food and drink experience is necessary', and are not content to accept for themselves and their followers an opinion concerning which the generality of men are completely unanimous, to say nothing of the *élite*. For if everything which is ascertained is ascertained only by the logos, and nothing is ascertained by experience, how is it possible that the generality, who do not use the logos, can know anything of what is known? And how was it that this was unamimously asserted among the elder physicians, not only by Hippocrates, but also by all those who came after him, Diogenes, Diocles, Praxagoras, Philotimos, and Erasistratos? For all of these acknowledge that what they know concerning medical practice they know by means of the logos in conjunction with experience. In particular, Diogenes and Diocles argue at length that there is no way of

ascertaining the ultimate disposal of food and drink except by experience. This was a matter on which Hippocrates had already pronounced a
definite judgement by stating that it was one of the things which are to be
ascertained by experience. And again, if you go back to Praxagoras and
Philotimos and Erasistratos, you will find that, even if they have made
more concessions to the logos than the older physicians have done
(though they are in confusion over several matters, such as that purslane
is a cure for tooth-ache and similar things), they confess that knowledge
of these things is to be discovered by experience, and that they enter into
dispute only with respect to those things which are more various and are
more mixed and complex than these. You may think, perhaps, that Herophilos—for he is the only one left of the afore-named and well-known
witnesses—was of a different opinion. And he is a man who is known by
everybody to have surpassed the great majority of the Ancients, not only
in width of knowledge but in intellect, and to have advanced the art of
medicine in many ways; as, for instance, by his logos on the pulsation of
veins, which one needs more now and finds more useful than any other
logos, for deriving benefit therefrom, while those before overlooked it
and neglected to investigate it. We find, however, that this Herophilos

110   concedes no small importance to experience, nay indeed, to speak the
truth (and it is the fittest to be spoken), he makes experience all-impor-
tant. And do you, fellow, bid me leave aside all these authorities and turn
to Asclepiades and consider what he says, when he is a man touched by
madness, who is well known and pointed out as a man who forgets his
own arguments and never remembers what he has uttered. Is it not he
who says: The physician Petron gave the sick roast meat to eat and wine
to drink? And that this had been found and discovered by the physicians
who lived before him, but it was he (scil. Asclepiades) later who ascertained the reason why this diet could benefit one who was treated by it.
And since this is Asclepiades' own statement, you may, in spite of the
other admissions of theirs for which you reproach them, regard this also
as a matter to accept from them by their avowal of it, namely that it is
possible to use an excellent remedy and not know its cause, for this is
what Asclepiades himself has admitted; he who was not content to say
that empiricism does not suffice and is inadequate, but also says it has no
certainty and no consistency. And the fact that he took over a method of
treating and healing from Petron without knowing the cause thereof. The
same thing was previously admitted by Erasistratos also, who used to
praise his master Chrysippos for his methods of treating and healing, but
did not extol his opinions on causes. And since this applies to all of these,
to whom can we now go and ask for further testimony? It is quite clear
that we must seek only for those things which are plain and open to

examination. And we for our part find that the things which are plain and open to examination are many and various in all the activities of men and in the other arts.

Chapter XIV

Since, however, you are dull of heart and blind of eye by reason of your anxiety to give good reasons for your opinions, it would perhaps be most fitting and just in our argument with you to take our proofs from things you yourselves avow. And I know you admit that you cannot state, whether in the case of poisonous animals or of the medicaments that give relief, or of deadly and life-saving medicaments, why this medicament relieves yellow bile and that phlegm, why this other eases thinness of the blood and the pains of jaundice and that black bile, nor why this is a remedy for two or more of these things, and that relieves them all, in a manner similar to the relaxing effect of the white cardamom. And you cannot tell why the castor passes through all the members of the body without harming them, but if it reaches the lungs it injures them alone, and why the Spanish fly is harmful to the bladder only. And likewise with respect to all the other poisons (pharmaka!) you can say nothing except that you can none the less sufficiently heal these diseases and disorders, and relieve and constrict the body if you should need to do so. And since this is the case, then you admit that you know these things only by experience, and this is a conclusion to which you are inevitably forced. Since there are only two things by means of which something can be ascertained, namely experience and conclusion from the visible to the invisible, and since by conclusion from the visible to the invisible nothing can be discovered in the matters which we have mentioned, even according to your own views, apart from the opinion of others, then nothing remains but that it is experience which can elicit what is required in these matters. I think now it is plain and obvious to all that the arguments used by the Dogmatists against the Empiricists, and with which they oppose empiricism, are refuted and shown to be erroneous.

Chapter XV

And here is another point of view, from which you, who vent your malice on us like a jaundiced maniac, may learn that you attack us unjustly. I

assert it to be unanimously admitted that there are remedies which have
been discovered by experience without any logos. Therefore I turn to you
and ask you to tell me in what manner knowledge of those things that
were discovered by experience without the logos became 'technical'
knowledge in which you have confidence? Did you place confidence in it
and accept it as 'technical' just because you had seen each single one of
these things take place once, or after you had discovered that it happened
112   many times? For my part I do not think that even if you were mad you
would say: We have placed our confidence in it, and in our opinion it is
'technical' knowledge, since we have seen that it has happened once. For
things which are visible fall into four classes: one of them is always plain,
another generally so, in the case of another lucidity and obscurity are
equally balanced, and the fourth is rarely plain. If then something visible
to the eye is seen only once, this single observation will not suffice to
indicate which of the four kinds of medical science it belongs to. Since
we do not know that it will appear on every future occasion as it has
done on this occasion, how should we know that it is always thus? Therefore it is not possible for us after having seen a thing once to be able to
foretell that what was seen on this occasion will often be seen, and that
its opposite will only be seen rarely, just as it is not possible to know
whether the reverse is the case. And since this belongs to what cannot be
recognized by a single observation, so in the case of both what is more
frequent and what is rare it is impossible to know the thing after seeing it
only once, and likewise it is not possible for that thing to be known
whose nature consists (both) in its being and in its not being
(amphidoxos).

And in short, if anyone says that what has been seen once deserves
acceptance, belief, and confidence, then he is not in a position to mistrust
or reject that which is seen many times, on the ground that, in his opinion, it belongs to that which is not credible and worthy of belief. And if
he constructs his logos on what has been seen once, and this in itself is
credible enough for him to place confidence in it, on condition, however,
that he requires to see those things a second time where conclusions
appear doubtful or unknown, then by Allah, I assure you that he will of
necessity require to see them a third, fourth, fifth, and sixth time. I assert
that experience has shown that what has produced a like result in three
cases can produce the reverse in three others. I say that a thing seen may
be seen exactly as before, and yet belong to those things which are of
both kinds (amphidoxos), or to those things which happen often, or to
those things which take place but rarely. It is obvious to all that it may be
113   seen only thus and yet belong to those things which happen

amphidoxos.* But you shall soon learn when I explain it to you that it is not impossible that it should belong to the things which are frequent or those which are rare, and yet can be seen in this manner. Consider: What is to prevent the medicine which is being tested from having a given effect on two hundred people and the reverse effect on twenty others, and that of the first six people who were seen at first and on whom the remedy took effect, three belong to the three hundred and three to the twenty without your being able to know which three belong to the three hundred, and which to the twenty, even if you were a sooth-sayer? And you surely do not say that you construct your logos on this. Since you are in this position, you must needs wait until you see the seventh and the eighth, or to put it shortly, very many people in succession.

Why** then, do you still continue with your slander, say that experience is incoherent, claim that "very many times" is indefinite and that it is unclear where it comes to a halt? In saying that you do not see where, do you believe to refute us rather than yourself? For it seems to me that you rather refute yourself. For there are two questions. One is whether something is found out by a single observation. I think that this is so and you agree, unwillingly, but nevertheless. The other question is how it is found out by a single observation. This question, I think, admits of no answer and is of no use. Hence it should be up to you to accomplish this remaining task to find out how. But, in claiming that this is a matter of controversy, you will refute yourself and do us no harm. For, what is at issue between us is not how what is technical comes about, but only whether it does come about. But we evidently agree on the fact that it does come about. And since you are the one who busies himself with causes, it is only fair that you should find out how it comes about. But you seem to do the opposite of what one ought to do and to behave just like those who, just because they do not understand how they see, do not agree that they do see, or who, just because they do not understand in which way what is coming into being comes into being, what passes away passes away and what moves is in motion, do away with coming into being, passing away, and motion. But who does not know that the greatest confusion of any reasoning lies in its conflict with what is evident? For how could a reasoning, which does not even get off to a start without evidence, be trustworthy, if it rails against the evidence from which it took its starting points? This is what Democritus knew, too, when he maligned the phenomena. Having said "by convention there is

114

---

* half of the time

**This section down to the end of the chapter again is extant in Greek and hence was not translated by Walzer.

colour, by convention there is sweetness, by convention there is bitterness, in truth there are just atoms and a void", he lets the senses speak to
the mind in this way "wretched mind, taking your evidence from us you
overthrow us? Our overthrow is your downfall." You should, then,
charge reason with being untrustworthy, since it is so devious that when
it is most convincing it is in conflict with the phenomena which served as
its basis. Instead you do the opposite: things for which you have* no
account of how they come to be you judge not to be, as reason demands.
But to me this very fact seems to be the most important objection to reason. For who in his mind can still trust reason when it comes to matters
which are not evident, if it is devious as to postulate the contrary of what
is obvious.

Chapter XVI

According to what is demanded by the logos, there must not be such a
thing in the world as a heap of grain, a mass or satiety, neither a mountain, nor strong love, nor a row, nor strong wind, nor city, nor anything
else which is known from its name and idea to have a measure of extent
or multitude, such as the wave, the open sea, a flock of sheep and herd of
cattle, the nation and the crowd. And the doubt and confusion introduced
by the logos leads to contradiction of fact in the transition of man from
one stage of his life to another, and in the changes of time, and the
115   changes of seasons. For in the case of the boy one is uncertain and doubtful as to when the actual moment arrives for his transition from boyhood
to adolescence, and in the case of the youth when he enters the period of
manhood, also in the case of the man in his prime when he begins to be
an old man. And so it is with the seasons of the year when winter begins
to change and merges into spring, and spring into summer, and summer
into autumn. By the same reasoning, doubt and confusion enter into
many other things which relate to the doings of men in spite of the fact
that knowledge of these things is obvious and plain. There are some
Dogmatists and logicians who call the argument expressing this doubt
'sorites' after the matter which first gave rise to this question, I mean the
heap. Other people call it the argument of little by little. They have only
named it thus in accordance with its method which leads to doubt and
confusion. And he who knows what kind of an argument this is has more
than enough of it in this discussion. Since, however, my opinion of you is

*reading "echontes"

that you are ignorant of the strength and bearing of this argument—were this not so, you would never have dared use it on an occasion so unsuitable—I would therefore question you in the very way by which you, in employing it, tried to demonstrate that seeing a thing very many times does not imply 'technical' knowledge. Now the first thing I would question you on is the heap; afterwards I shall ask you about all the other things.

CHAPTER XVII

Wherefore I say: tell me, do you think that a single grain of wheat is a heap? Thereupon you say: No. Then I say: What do you say about 2 grains? For it is my purpose to ask you questions in succession, and if you do not admit that 2 grains are a heap then I shall ask you about 3 grains. Then I shall proceed to interrogate you further with respect to 4 grains, then 5 and 6 and 7 and 8, and you will assuredly say that none of these makes a heap. Also 9 and 10 and 11 grains are not a heap. For the conception of a heap which is formed in the soul and is conjured up in the imagination is that, besides being single particles in juxtaposition, it has quantity and mass of some considerable size. In my opinion, therefore, you would not be at fault were you to declare that 100 grains even would not be what men may call a heap, despite the fact that it has quantity which may be taken in one's hand. I appreciate your caution and foresight here in speaking thus, but shall interogate you further all the same: would you allow 101 grains of wheat to be called a heap? I think you will again say: No. Then I would have you tell me: What do you say with regard to grains whose number has reached 102? I know that here, too, you will not affirm it. And again I would ask you: what do you think of grains whose number is now 103? You will say: No. And concerning the grains whose number has reached 104? And you will say: Not yet. And then I shall ask you: And the grains whose number amounts to 105? You will answer: Assuredly not. I for my part shall not cease from continuing to add one to the number in like manner, nor desist from asking you without ceasing if you admit that the quantity of each single one of these numbers constitutes a heap. I shall proceed to explain the cause of this. If you do not say with respect to any of the numbers, as in the case of the 100 grains of wheat for example, that it now constituted a heap, but afterwards when a grain is added to it, you say that a heap has now been formed, consequently this quantity of corn became a heap by the addition of the single grain of wheat, and if the grain is taken away the

16

heap is eliminated. And I know of nothing worse and more absurd than
that the being and not-being of a heap is determined by a grain of corn.
And to prevent this absurdity from adhering to you, you will not cease
from denying, and will never admit at any time that the sum of this is a
heap, even if the number of grains of wheat reaches infinity by the constant and gradual addition of more. And by reason of this denial the heap
is proved to be non-existent, because of this pretty sophism. And so it
follows necessarily from this sophism that the mountain also does not
exist. Tell me, do you think that the being and not-being of the mountain
is determined by a single ell? The question which I shall ask you concerning it consists of two questions, because I wish to capture you from
two sides. Let me ask you, first, if a hill can attain a height above the level
117   of the ground which would justify its being called a mountain, and you
were to take one ell from its height, would it no longer be a mountain?
You say: No. Then let me say: I do not believe that you will say that a
level spot on the ground or an elevation which rises but an ell above the
ground must be called a mountain. For the conception in the mind and
the image in the soul is that a mountain is something which is of large
dimensions and has height and a considerable measure of size, not that it
is something very small in size. And were this not the case, then every
place would be a mountain. Now see, if we are agreed on these things,
how it can be shown by this argument that there is no such thing as a
mountain. For we would further ask: Do you believe that the mound
which rises 2 ells above the ground is a mountain? And you answer: It is
by no means a mountain. Then we would say to you: And what do you
state about a mound which is 3 ells in height? That you will again say 'no'
is perfectly clear and plain. And we say to you: And the mound which is
4 ells above the ground? Again you say: No. And we say to you: And as
to the mound which is 5 ells above the surface of the earth, do you call
that a mountain? And we know that all men say: This, too, is not a mountain. It is the same with regard to the hills which are higher than these, I
mean those which are 6 or 7 or 9 ells high. But I do not let you go, nor do
I break off my questioning, but cause the hill to grow perpetually by adding ell to ell. And since you have already admitted from the very first that
it is not possible by adding an ell to make a mountain of that which was
not a mountain before and that which was a mountain before is not pre-
vented from remaining one by the removal of an ell, and since in no way
whatsoever or at any time can you admit that it has now become a mountain, I shall proceed in my argument to make the hill so high that its measure will reach a milliard ells. Even then you will not be able to say that it
is a mountain, to say nothing of another (elevation), in order not to fall
into the absurdity of saying that what to begin with you did not venture

to call a mountain, did become a mountain, because of an ell you had added to it. For you would then have given a single ell such force that by its addition the object to which it was added became a mountain, and by its subtraction was no mountain. When we question you and fall into confusion about the hills whose elevation above the earth's surface is so great, and yet we cannot say they are mountains, how much more will you be confused and embarrassed in the case of each of the other hills and refuse to say it is a mountain.

118

The second result of this admirable argument, which follows the first, is that we find there is no such thing as a mountain, and then a third and fourth and fifth and sixth result show that there is no row, no city and no flock, no army, no crowd and no nation, for not one of these is formed by the union of one or two things which causes this to become a people, and this a row, and this a flock, and this an army, and this something else, but rather because a union of many individuals must take place, if one wishes this to be a row of people and that, a nation, also that not an inconsiderable number of sheep must come together if one wishes to call this collection a flock, and not a few houses are necessary if one wishes their conglomeration to constitute a city. I would ask of you to tell me how many men are in an army, and how many houses are necessary to form a city, and how many sheep constitute a flock, and of how many people a nation must consist. And you know that if I were to take each single unit of these categories and increase their number by adding one unit at a time, you would say that there is no nation in the world, no army, and no city. Were it not so, you would perforce have to affirm the existence of each one of these as well as its non-existence, by reason of one single unit which is either added to or subtracted from it. If, however, each single unit of each one of these does not yet form its whole, I mean neither nation, nor row, nor flock, because they are things whose number is large, or whose measure is one of the things which we cannot find nor reach by investigation, you would be acting both unjustly and wrongly in pestering us to specify, of a thing which when seen once only is not 'technical' according to your argument, how many times it must be seen in order to become 'technical'. As if we could not turn the question against you and say: If the single grain of wheat is not a heap, how many grains form a heap? Or if one individual is not a row, how many individuals make a row, or how many are in an army, or what number forms a nation, or how large is a flock?

119

Do you impute this against us because we cannot state with exactitude the precise number contained in each of these, but are only able to give a general notion of what they are and of what is formed of each of them in the mind or in the imagination? Since each has always been capable of expansion and augmentation and without limit or end at which its being stops, it is therefore impossible for us to say how large is the number of each one of them. If you wish, speak, it will not cause me to be angry with you; if, however, you should say of something which people continually see under the same conditions throughout their lives, that it is nonexistent, it will not help you at all. For you reject it and declare it to be invalid only by the logos, but not in reality, since you only contradict yourself and prove yourself in the wrong. Since, however, every logos is bad if contradicted by one single point in a thing that is plain to the senses, consequently yours is a bad and a wrong logos. And how should this not be the worst and most erroneous of all logoi, since so many facts contradict it?

CHAPTER XVIII

I for my part adhere to and follow that which is known to men, and accept what is obvious without inquiring into the cause of each individual thing. Therefore I say of what has been seen but once, that it is not 'technical', just as the single grain of wheat is not a perfect heap; if, however, it is a thing that is seen many times in the same way, then I call it 'technical'. For I observe that children, too, do not learn to write on hearing and seeing the letters of the alphabet only once, but they must hear and see them many times. How many times they must do so I shall not ask, since I gain no advantage thereby. You, however, prompted by your dilettantism in seeking to investigate what is neither useful nor necessary, trouble yourself with this and all other (like) matters. If you should wish to inquire here too how we become expert and technical (technikoi) when we have seen the thing very many times, you will find that your own words reflect upon yourself, and place the burden of proof on you. Pray tell us how did the mousikos—he it is who makes melodies—learn the sounds of the melody? Do you say that he learned them when he heard them for the first time, or after he had accustomed himself to them very many times? Or how did he learn the measure, the beat, and the various kinds of sounds? Why are you not able after hearing two sounds to recognize the measure of difference between them with respect to sharpness and depth, while he who has been thoroughly trained in the recognition of the different kinds of sounds is able to do so? Probably he who can tell the measure exactly can find nothing else to say except that he has practised himself in it very frequently. Surely you see that those youths who are apprenticed to masters become masters themselves only in the same

120

way, the one learning how copper is engraved, another how wood is planed, and another how leather is cut and in what manner of cutting. And after each apprentice has seen very many times how these things are done, and this is given him as an aim to be accomplished in a 'technical' way, he strives to fashion something with his own hands, but he is not yet a master and skilled craftsman until he has practised that work very many times with his own hands in the same way. If he does so, long experience will make him an expert master, because the knowledge of the master and of the expert and the 'technician' can only be attained and perfected in this way, little by little in an imperceptible increase. And everyone knows that this can only happen after many single manipulations. But as to how often these indispensable preliminary works must be done nothing plain and definite can be said by anybody. Likewise in the case of goldsmiths and painters: they become masters after long experience and a thorough training of the vision.

Again, the Dogmatist says: Assuredly you have made clear very many other things which were hitherto false and absurd, but you have failed to show how something after it has been seen very many times can become 'technical', composed as it is of many things each of which has been seen once, and consequently cannot be 'technical'. I should accordingly answer him thus: I have not enlarged upon your absurdity; the thing, however, of which you accuse me has been refuted, and as for the fallacious arguments you have brought forward, they have been clearly shown to refute your own argument, and have caused the case to go against you. I say all this because in the way men live, and in all their activities and all arts, and also from the logical conclusion of your own argument, it has been found that what has been seen many times becomes 'technical'. With regard to the cause, however, which makes it completely 'technical' and when it begins to be completely 'technical', I am of opinion that it is idle to demand this. For I find that not a particle of harm befalls arts and men in their modes of life and activities for being ignorant of such things. If you wish to question and argue about it then, whether you find answers which will solve your questions, or whether you find none, in either case you do not harm me in the very least, but you undoubtedly harm yourself. Should you find solutions to your questions, then you may be sure that the answers you receive are vain, and that you only refute yourself by falling into error and by separating yourself from the truth. And if you should get no answer to your questions, you have no right to reproach us or make a charge against us that the fact does not exist, for it is assuredly clear that it does exist. If, however, you cannot explain the cause of its existence, then you cannot believe in any of the visible things, to say nothing of others. Once this

121

has been made clear, then no person in his senses could be persuaded by the arguments brought forward by the logos. And yet do you command me not to believe that which is evident to the senses, since I cannot explain how a thing is truly 'technical' that has been observed very many times? I am no Sophist whose business it is to refute errors, or to compound them and form a chain of them. Nor am I such a fool as to believe all you say on the spot and without hesitation.

CHAPTER XIX

I find, too, many other things which by the argument of the logos and your reasoning are quite unknown, but which we nevertheless must not avoid and hold aloof from because they have a being which is not evident. If this is not the case, pray tell me: wherefore do you return to belief in that which is evident to the senses when you cannot refute what is said concerning movement, mixtures, and many other things? For example in the case of bodies which are mixed with each other, either the one must permeate the other, or they must combine together by way of juxtaposition. The theory which holds it to be inacceptable that the substance should be dissolved and the separation of its parts brought about holds also that those who say that composite bodies are conjoined with each other by being placed in juxtaposition must [not] be regarded as reliable. For the exponents of the former view assert that whoever says this must inevitably be led to deny the existence of God and His providence for His creation, and the substance of the soul and the substance of nature specific to both. But these are things the enormity and unsurpassable absurdity of which we need not mention. As for the view that composite bodies are permeated the one by the other, although nothing remains except this, yet it is something which one cannot easily imagine, and I am far from thinking of it, to say nothing of understanding it and knowing it. For that two bodies, or three and often four or five, should occupy the same place is a condition difficult to imagine and to think of, although there is no other possibility except that one or other of these is the truth. And the fact itself is one of those facts which are almost clearly evident.

Let us leave this now and reflect upon that which concerns the universe, and consider what may be said about it, whether it is originated or not originated, for one or other of these statements must be the truth, there being no third thing between the two which the imagination can form a picture of. Which of the two, however, is the truth is by no means

122

ascertainable; for if someone says it is not originated, his statement is refuted by the conclusion which inevitably follows from this that God did not create the world, although He did create man, also that His providence cannot possibly extend through endless ages. And the third (conclusion which logically follows from this view) along with these two is that the world continues to exist without requiring in any way the providence of God at all. For if the universe is not originated, it is in no danger of decay, nor is it open to chance happenings and disorders, because there is no need to fear that a thing which has absolutely no beginning to its being and origin will ever decay; and in this case it has no need of anyone (*i.e.* God) to uphold it, or to secure and direct it. Whoso believes, however, that the world is originated is forced to the following conclusion: if there were a time when the universe did not yet exist, then God either of his own will neglected to do what was best and most perfect or else He was not capable of accomplishing this thing and was not able to do it. The expression of either of these views is blasphemy and is not permissible to him who utters them. For the assertion that God withheld Himself from doing what is best, and left matter alone without wishing to organize and arrange it, is to accuse Him of utter slackness and negligence. If He had wished it, but could not accomplish it, this would be a sign of powerlessness and weakness on His part. In the same way the argument by which motion is contradicted is of such difficulty as to cause the Dogmatists and dialecticians who concern themselves with this much trouble and distress when they seek to refute it. I do not think that this escapes your notice or is concealed from you. But many of our party—but I need not say 'of our party' because practically everybody with the exception of a few think as we do—do not listen at all, either sleeping or waking, to the answer to these fallacies and to their refutation, yet they have no doubt as to the fact of motion, and have in general no idea of the fallacies and the arguments against them, since they cannot detach themselves from that which is evident to the senses in any way whatsoever.

123

CHAPTER XX

The dilemma which results from the logos describing the heap is much more absurd than the dilemma with regard to motion, and you may think that you can turn the argument against us by making use of this sorites, and so plunge us into doubt and confusion, if that which is not yet in the category of what has been seen very many times, but has been seen only a few times or has been seen many times without the many times being

124   very frequent, then, when the experience of a single time is added, comes
into the category of what has been seen very many times. O you, who
never cease imagining vain things, are not other things made plain by
these words and by just these very arguments, as in the first instance, that
by adding an ounce of water to something it becomes a sea, and secondly, that something which was not heavy becomes heavy on the weight
of a drachm being added to it? If, again, you were to augment and
increase the measure of water ounce by ounce and were to increase and
augment the measure of the thing that is weighed drachm by drachm
there inevitably ensues for you one of two conclusions: either you do not
say at one time or other that the water is now a sea, or that this thing is
heavy, or that you undoubtedly see yourself driven to confess that the
water has become a sea by the addition of one ounce, and that the thing
which is weighed has become heavy by the addition of the weight of one
drachm. But the Dogmatist says: True, yet nevertheless I do not understand how it can be that the thing seen 100 times, for instance, without
having for all that reached the stage of having-been-seen-very-many-
times, now because of having being seen a single time, belongs to what
has been seen very many times. I confront you here and say: I, too, do
not understand how a man becomes bald because of a single wisp of hair.
I use the instance of a bald-headed man because you are worthy of hearing and receiving this and similar things. I do not know if there is anything more deserving of ridicule than this, I mean, that a man becomes
bald because a single wisp of hair falls from his head. Your argument,
however, circles round this very point, and implies precisely this. Now
reflect how this that I have said to you is necessitated. I say: A hair falls
from someone's head, then a second follows, then a third, a fourth, and
many other hairs in succession. Now I would ask you on the falling out
of each of these hairs one after the other: Has the man now become bald?
You will then inevitably have to make one of two answers: either you
reject the statement and steadily refuse to admit that he is becoming
bald, even if all his hair were to fall out, or, should this be quite impossible, when, pray, does he then become bald? Your first assertion would

125   logically involve his becoming bald on the falling out of a single hair. For
since you did not say he was bald before a single hair fell from his head,
and when this single hair did fall out you said he had become bald, and
called him by this name, then I think, or rather I do not doubt that you
said he was bald owing to the loss of a single hair only. For my part, I
know of nothing more absurd and stupid than (to say) that a man
becomes bald on a single hair falling from his head, and that his hair
becomes luxuriant if a single tuft is added to it. This argument and this
proof and that argument and that proof are what you people have

brought forward in order to refute our argument about what has been seen very many times. Similar, too, is the other argument which follows the first and runs thus. Tell me, to whom may the term boy be applied, and when does the moment arrive for the boy to become a man? I purpose now to begin my contention with you on this point with the 13th year so as not to trouble you too much. Wherefore I would ask you: Does the boy on having attained this year and one day still remain a boy? Undoubtedly you will agree with me on this point. Then I would proceed to ask you about 13 and two days? On your agreeing to this, I would then question further in like manner, enumerating the days in succession, making mention of the third and fourth and fifth day and of those that follow. I think you have seen and understood whither your fallacious arguments will lead you. For either you make the boy into a youth by the addition of one day, or else if you fear and avoid doing so, you will not say he is a youth, even if in the meantime he were to reach the age of 30 by adding one day to the other. And you are placed in the same dilemma in the case of the youth entering manhood. At this point you are already aware of the dilemma in which you are placed when adding day to day. And if I, in the course of my addition, add hour to hour, you will, I am sure, understand more plainly and more thoroughly the absurdity and enormity of these arguments of yours. For just as that man became bald because one single hair fell from his head, although he was not bald before, so here because of a single hour this youth becomes an old man. There is nothing more absurd and stupid than this, that a person who an hour before a certain moment was but a youth should an hour later have become an old man. In like manner seasons and lands, distance and proximity, many and little are eliminated and reduced to nothing.

126

And this logos never ceases to advance until it reaches the state of that physical imagination and conceptual phantasy which is called universal and forms a part of what is public and universally known. Thus one who has not seen the city of Alexandria believes that there is in Egypt a town called Alexandria; he does not, however, believe this on hearing of it from one single person or from two people, but after he has heard of it from a larger number of people. Now, I would ask you to tell me how many people would he have to listen to before believing that the town existed? Would you say three or four or five? After that I shall not cease from adding to the number one by one and asking you until I force you to say that the thing which you formerly asserted was not to be credited has now become credible by the addition of a single unit. In all these categories and questions, if you answer them and rebut them, you are answering and rebutting on our behalf, justifying(?) us, bringing victory to our argument and defending it. If you are not able to do so and cannot

rebut and answer them, what made you then demand an answer from us
to a question containing a fallacy which logically involves everyone, and
constrain us to answer it, particularly as I am no Sophist and do not
belong to those whose business, aim, and intention it is to confute fallacious arguments and reject them? What we have hitherto done in the
matter is only what you have called upon us to do and involved us in
against our will. You have diverted us from that which is useful to us, by
forcing us to repel the injustice directed against us by you, and the hostil-
ity you nourish against us. Thus it is perfectly clear from the other crafts
and from all the occupations by which men gain a livelihood, and also in
accordance with your own views, that what is known by experience
alone, is not outside the domain of the logos and logic.

CHAPTER XXI

127

As for the other proposition, that put forward by the Dogmatists, it has
now been discredited and discovered to be an argument whose outcome
and conclusion is the opposite of their aim and views. For its aim and
object was to disparage and depreciate empiricism and to prove that it
does not advance along 'technical' lines, and that it is neither credible nor
reliable, But now it itself has been discredited and exposed and found to
be unreliable to the extent that what is most convincing in it is manifestly
opposed to the things which lie open to perception by the senses. And
you, too, O Dogmatists, admit that many conceptions are elicited by
experience. We, however, shall now prove to you by this method which
we are pursuing that experience has not only discovered simple conceptions in simple cases, but that through experience alone there can be discovered also subtle and most complicated conceptions in the matters
which are the subject of your own argument.

Pray tell us to what logos can you attribute it, and what arguments can
you bring forward for the statement that these additions of four (days) at
a time continue in very acute diseases for twenty days and then come to
an end? Tell us further, why the beginning of the third week is not the
fifteenth day—as the beginning of the second week is the eighth day—but
is the fourteenth day, and why the day which prognosticates the twenti-
eth day is the seventeenth day, and why three weeks last until the twenti-
eth day and end there and not on the twenty-first? Why is bleeding of the
nose salutary if it comes from the nostril on the affected side, but injuri-
ous if the bleeding is on the other side? Why, too, are things of a red colour less in number? If in these cases and in many others in which, even

according to your own opinion, there is much subtlety and complexity you have no argument of proof or cause to which to attribute them, you stand discredited and the speciousness of your fallacies is revealed. As for the most capable Asclepiades, he (admits)—although we for our part do not exalt(?) him or support him by saying, according to his wish, that what he says is the truth, when he prescribes for the sick wine to drink and meat to eat, both things which he particularly boasts of—that they have been discovered by experience alone.

128

CHAPTER XXII

Perhaps you are still doubtful, O Dogmatist, about the third of the three arguments with which you attack our doctrine, and still adhere to your position and your views on it, namely that the Empiricist cannot retain everything in his memory because the multiplicity of things goes beyond the limits of finiteness. If you persist in such an attitude you will force me to mention the words of Diogenes, who said, on an Athenian (?) setting him the riddle by which motion is eliminated, the sum and substance of his argument being that there is no such thing as motion: 'I am surprised at these miserable seafarers who annoy us all day long with their cries of: Who is going to Rhodes, who to Cnidos, to Kos, to Lesbos?'.

I say the same now: I am surprised, since the diseases are endless and their symptoms too are endless, and the changing of their order is not 'technical', how you, Asclepiades, the most excellent of all men, have contrived to write three treatises on acute diseases and to imagine that, although you have left nothing unsaid in them, either about the symptoms which precede the disease (i.e. the prognostical symptoms) or about the symptoms which appear along with it (i.e. the diagnostical symptoms), or about the symptoms which follow it (i.e. the therapeutic symptoms), you have thereby united in your book the causes of diseases and their remedies, seeing that their number is endless; while Diogenes writing more briefly and compendiously than you has collected the diseases and their causes and remedies in one treatise, and Praxagoras wrote two treatises on symptoms which appear along with the diseases; likewise Hippocrates wrote two treatises on diseases. How is it that you have been granted the sovereign power to establish in your book all the symptoms which adhere to and affect conjointly one who suffers from phrenitis, as being symptoms belonging to a single person, while I have not this power, but because of me the phrenetic becomes not one but many, for they differ in respect of ages, lands, seasons, and physical conditions,

129 activities, and temperaments? I should very much like to know your opinion. Do you maintain that Socrates was not one but many, because when he lived in the city he was other than when he was in the army, or when he tarried in the shade he was other than when he was in the sun? Or do you think that he was Socrates in the winter and became someone else in the summer? Would you say he was Socrates when he was young, but on becoming old he was no longer Socrates but Pythagoras; or perhaps you would say that so long as he did not go to the baths he was Socrates, but on bathing he was Socrates no longer? And when he was asleep, your assertion is that he was other than when he was awake; and when he was thirsty he was other than when he had drunk? Or perhaps this is all idle talk and vain chatter, since Socrates was not Socrates only because he bathed, or because he was armed or unarmed, or because he was young or old, or because it was winter or summer, but it was because of something else apart from all this that Socrates was Socrates? For as long as that essential thing remains unchanged it is clear that even if the whole of his other circumstances were to be changed, he would not be affected in the very least in respect of being Socrates; for even if the qualities which were in him and from which in respect of being Socrates he derived no advantage (yet because of which he was fitted to be Socrates) were to be stripped away, that would not harm him. Since the case is as I have described, how can you refuse to admit that this also applies to the phrenetic? For if he had phrenitis because it is winter, he would not have it in summer, or if he had phrenitis on a full stomach, he would not have it on an empty one. And if he had phrenitis in respect of gathering flowers and picking roses and grass(?) and raving and uttering senseless words and feverishness, then there is amongst the other characteristics not one which would justify his being called phrenetic by attributing it to him, nor would it harm him in respect of not being phrenetic by denying it to him.

Since matters are thus, then the phrenetic, if he is not called so because he is this or that, but is only called phrenetic because all these symptoms have come together and are found in him, then his therapy is the one which is peculiar to his case, I mean the pouring of a certain liq-

130 uid over his head, and his being treated in the manner suited to him. For even if he should need blood-letting he will need it, not in so far as he is a phrenetic, but in so far as he is strong and young, just as if these two things were to happen together in other illnesses of his and he needed an emptying of the body; for the necessity of emptying in the case of bodies which are plethoric—that is bodies in which there are many humours—is to preserve a single uncompounded thing in a single uncompounded case. For this reason, when both things appear together, I mean the total-

ity of the symptoms which in their union point to plethora and the totality of the symptoms which in their union point to phrenitis, we apply
blood-letting and empty this one particular body, in so far as it is plethoric, and treat it in so far as it suffers from phrenitis in that manner
suited to the case, by pouring over the head those liquids which are
poured over the head of one suffering from such a disease. This in
accordance with what we remember about the healing of the phrenetic.

If they assert in the case of a healthy man and in the case of one to
whom anything in general happens, whatever it may be, that he consists
of many, we cannot fail to be surprised at their judgement. For if this
were the case, then the regulations issued by law-givers, according to
which those people who do good gain praise and honour, while people
who do what is bad receive admonition and punishment, are useless and
absurd, because it is not just nor right that he who is now honoured and
rewarded because of a good deed is a different person from the one who
has performed any kind of good work, by means of which he deserved
just these very benefits, and that he is rewarded with a reward of which
he was unworthy, and it is neither right nor just that this man be pun-
ished and admonished, since he is no longer the man he originally was,
when he committed evil and did wrong.

Chapter XXIII

I have, however, heard them speak of that which in itself is a single thing
as being of two species. One of them is something in which a symptom
shows itself, and is grasped by means of sensation, and the other is
something in which there is nothing additional to, and no diminution of,
the thing itself. This second species either does not exist in the manner   131
asserted by the majority of them, or, if it does exist, it must not be sought
in bodies, And if there is no thing of this second kind which is a single
thing in itself, and if in the second kind a thing exists which in itself is a
single thing, there are, inevitably, but two possible conclusions for you to
arrive at: either that you do not admit at some time or other that something is a single thing in itself, or that you say precisely what we say
about it. If you say what we say, why blame us then, and accuse us of
absurdity? And if you at some time or other do not say that something is
a single thing in itself, you turn the argument against yourself and justify
our accusation against you. Nothing, however, of all this refutes my argument even if no thing at all in any signification which can be described
were a single thing in itself along with another. Why fill your books in

vain with chapters on the diagnosis of diseases or chapters on their treatment, if nothing of what you write about can be seen?

The assertion of the Dogmatists that by means of the logos they can bring into unity things which are utterly opposed to each other gives one cause for the greatest astonishment at the excellence of their intelligence. If I but knew whether they are after things which we believe to be many and are not in reality a single thing, and which they then invert and revise and recreate in a new form and change until they become something which they are not, or whether it concerns things which are one in themselves, but which many people do not consider one! Do they themselves distinguish them and produce proofs that they are something different from the interpretation which gathers them into a unity, so that one thing could become different things? Naturally the Dogmatist answers: 'We make them one, although they are not uniform'. If he says this, his words do not fall far short of absolute ignorance and illiteracy in our view. If he says: 'This is according to the second way', we would answer: I should very much like to know if you are empowered to see the one thing which in itself is one, although it exists as a multiplicity and we are unable to do so.' Thereupon they say: 'Naturally, since you have no method of drawing a conclusion, with the help of which inferences are drawn from the visible to the invisible.' And when they say this to us, we would answer: 'You who possess this method of drawing conclusions have not even one single logos of this kind which is one and the same for all of you. Now since this is how matters stand with you, you are obliged to maintain according to this logos that any one of you who uses the inference from the visible to the invisible properly and according to rule, can write a chapter in a book on diagnosis of the conditions of a phrenetic, and a chapter on methods of healing it, treating it as a single phenomenon. But there is not one single one amongst all of you who is capable of doing so. Since these are the facts of the case, why return to your attack upon us, after having just agreed to make a thing in itself, one thing? Why oppose us when that which was elicited by inference from the visible to the invisible cannot possibly be something to which you all agree, because this conclusion in your opinion cannot be one and the same thing? And so it is not possible for you to diagnose the case of the phrenetic, treating it as a single phenomenon. If you should say you learn about this by means of another logos, then we should on no account reject this logos or refute it. For in my opinion there are two kinds of logoi: the one is called analogismos* and the other epilogis-

132

* analogism

mos*. We refuse, however, and reject only one of them, the one known as analogismos. My estimation of you, however, is that you deceive people and make a mock of them because you like them to honour and praise you for what you do not possess, and you are not ashamed of it, especially with regard to things into which your lack of education leads you to adventure, and you claim that many things are discovered by the logos. And should you be asked: What is this logos? You would answer: It is the thing called analogismos.

CHAPTER XXIV

I think that it would be better and more fitting for me to explain the difference between the two methods of drawing a conclusion. I shall not content myself with explaining them by saying in general terms that what is known as epilogismos is the conclusion pointing to visible things, and what is called analogismos is the conclusion pointing to invisible   133
things, but I shall show in detail in the case of single particular things how each of these methods is to be recognized.

I shall begin with the things wherein you agree with us in saying that he who discovers the categories of medical science discovers them and he who learns them learns them by explanations with commentary and summaries. I would say to you: You follow a path which is different from the path we are pursuing. You say first of all, it is necessary for the natural condition to be discovered, and he who does not know this will not succeed in recognizing the unnatural state of things. Then you inquire as to the manner in which man took his origin by the uniting of the elements which you claim to have discovered and found by first using the logos and investigation of the elements in order to discover this. Then you examine the functions and say this is of use in finding out and learning about the affected parts and the diseased organs of the body more easily and readily. For you assert that if one knows about the natural functions of a certain organ, it is easy, should that function be deranged, to understand something of what is necessary for the diseased organ. And should he know this, and know the salient cause, then there is no further difficulty; on the contrary, it is easy and a simple thing to find the method of healing which will eliminate this cause. I, for my part, think that if you proceed in this fashion, you are fittingly plunged into doubts and contradictions by inquiry into the elements, and also that you must

---

* epilogism

inevitably hold different opinions as to the natural functions, upon which there is no unanimity and agreement. Likewise too, there will be diversity of opinions with regard to disease in addition to (diversity of) opinion about functions. Each one of you affirms a doctrine which is different from the doctrine of the others, just because none of you are satisfied with one single universal doctrine. Respecting the inference known as epilogismos it is, as we say directed towards visible things, and is an inference common and universally used by the whole of mankind, and wherein men are unanimous, and where there is no such thing as schism and diversity of opinion. This is very fit and proper, since it has been well tested and rectified, because visible things testify to its correctness. Never at any time can it be divergent or confused or combine two contradictory things. Concerning the conclusion, however, which is called analogismos, because the invisible things cannot be perceived by the senses, the really sound argument does not become credible and the weak and mendacious argument cannot be shown up and destroyed. For this reason therefore, when differences of opinion arise with regard to an abscess in the bladder even before it becomes visible, a decision can be reached between them. For if we see an abscess appear after lancing with a lancet, then its appearance puts to shame him who says there is no abscess in the bladder, and proves his view to be wrong, and furnishes evidence that the opinion of the other people is correct; but if on lancing no abscess is to be seen, then the reverse is the case. In the same way stones in the bladder are tested empirically. Whether, however, the burning inflammation arising from the blood results from a hot substance which flows into the organ or from blood falling from the arteries and veins, or from things which cause violent heat and swelling, or that the atoms—these are parts which cannot be divided further—remain in the pores between the'veins, and whether the disease known as phrenitis arises from lesions of the brain itself, or from lesions of the membranes surrounding it, or from the integument; all these are instances of things which cannot possibly be proved to be true or wrong by means of any visible symptom. For this reason it is possible in the case of the one to arrive at a decision and to distinguish between the diversity of opinions, but not in the case of the other. And if you wish to know this, then consider how it is possible for us to decide the differences of opinion between these men, whether by perception of the senses—but how could this be possible since these are things which cannot be perceived by the senses—or by the logos and convincing words, for this is certainly better. But 'convincing' is only a relative conception and differs in the case of each individual, representing something that is non-specific with regard to the nature of the thing itself; but is specific with regard to the destruction and mischief in which peo-

134

ple who adhere to theories are involved. When, therefore, anyone   135
attempts to decide between people who hold diverse opinions with
regard to invisible things; only two possibilities are open to him: either
he is totally unprejudiced and impartial so that he remains suspended,
showing no inclination nor partisanship, or else he is one of those people
who hold a decided opinion, and allows himself to be deceived by his
own opinion, which inclines him to one of the opinions of those people
who refer to him as umpire. Everyone who accepts the office of umpire
inclines to something different from what the other inclines to, and in
this way schism and separation occur amongst them. For there are some
people amongst them, who are led to do so by their inclination to the sort
of thing that would carry conviction to Erasistratos; and so they praise
Erasistratos' view and reject the views of all other people, calling themselves for this reason Erasistrateans and band themselves together like
capable soldiers who are led by a single leader. Other people, again,
assert Praxagoras' view to be good and right; so you find that by their
belief in him they are convinced by what carried conviction to Praxagoras. A fitting motto for these persons would be what Homer said
about Odysseus: 'Greatly do we desire to be companies of Praxagoras,
the noble, the great-hearted' Then you will find a third army, the disciples of Asclepiades, and you will find other people who have made Herophilos their leader, master, and director in all their affairs, others again
accord Hippocrates this position. I am sure you will have understood—
unless you are utterly ignorant and superficial—that it is the conclusion
and the logos known as epilogismos if it is a logos universally known and
used, and a logos which they all employ, and concerning which there is
complete unanimity, and which refers to visible things alone. But if it is a
conclusion and a logos which only some individuals employ and use, and
which others regard as incorrect, and which refers to invisible things
only, then it is the conclusion and logos which men call analogismos.

Chapter XXV

Likewise in affirming what is necessitated by something that is said or
done, you will find two kinds of affirmation, one after the manner of the   136
logos known as epilogismos concerning which there is unanimity, and
the other after the manner of the logos known as analogismos concerning
which there is no unanimity.

Asclepiades, for instance, says it is not necessary and indeed not
advisable to apply blood-letting to one suffering from phrenitis. On

being asked the reason for this view, he says: 'Because this disease is due to the atoms not being found in their proper places in the pores of the cerbral membrane, and if you empty out the blood from the veins, it would not be of use in this disease, but would only weaken and diminish the strength (of the sick person).' Now when Asclepiades says this, I hear him make mention of the atoms and pores and of position in the cerebral membrane. This, however, is a view concerning invisible things, so his statement is one peculiar to himself, and is accepted and maintained by none but himself. Since this is the case with regard to his opinion, I must regard it as an analogismos. Then another comes along and says: 'I do not say that I know, nor that I reject or deny anything of that which this man says, because he speaks of things which are highly invisible, and if you wish to hear what in this case has been evident to the eye, not once, nor twice, but very many times, I shall describe it to you. For I have seen very many sufferers from phrenitis who were treated by blood-letting. Those of them who were young and strong benefited greatly therefrom, but the others derived but small benefit. Now if you were not to admit in your own mind that I and the other physicians are correct, then question them about it.' The Empiricist would say: 'Anyone hearing this opinion would recognize it at once as a statement concerning visible things, containing nothing peculiar to one person rather than another, and having nothing to do with invisible things.' Should he then go to the other physicians, and find that this is something wherein they all agree, then I do not doubt but that he will be led thereby to consider as correct the conclusion known as epilogismos which refers to visible things, and that he will prefer it to the conclusion known as analogismos which refers to invisible things.

137   Similarly, one of the physicians may say: 'A person suffering from the disease known as loss of memory (stupor) must not be spoken to, since his disease is due to inflammation of the cerebral membrane, and motion is not good for any inflamed organ.' This is a statement which belongs to the method known as analogismos since it deals with invisible things, and is a view which is asserted only by those who follow this method, and concerning which men are not all unanimous, and think the same about it. Then another comes and says: 'I have often observed that in every case when we sat by the bedside of a person sick of this disease which had him completely in his power and controlled him, if we did not rouse him and keep him awake, he was worse.' This is a statement which belongs to the method known as epilogismos. On the whole the conclusion known as epilogismos prescribes the doing of what should be done on the basis of the good or evil which is inherent in the thing and accompanies it, whereas the conclusion known as analogismos prescribes action

on the basis of the natures of things. If someone were to ask, for instance, what is the reason for not allowing the stretching of a luxation which is accompanied by a wound (? ulcer), the physician using the method known as analogismos would base his answer on an inquiry into the nature of the joints and sinews, and the substance of each one of them, as well as into the nature of this malady, and would then construct his argument as to what action and treatment he considered necessary on the basis of this investigation. As for the physician who uses the method known as epilogismos, he would say: The luxation which is accompanied by a wound must not be stretched, for were we to do so, the result would be convulsions and death. If anyone were to say to him: and why is this the case, his opinion would be that investigation into the causes of this is an unnecessary superfluity. Likewise anyone asking: why is dropsy—which is the gathering of water resulting from feverish complaints—such a serious disease, the Dogmatist would thereupon inquire into the nature and substance of fever and of the disease known as dropsy, and how it is originated in feverish diseases, and the reason for its being a serious complaint. The Empiricist, however, demands only a partial cause, and a relation of the symptoms which this disease brings in its train, and says: 'This kind of dropsy becomes serious because the fever does not leave the person suffering from it, besides the disease causes him to feel great pain, and torments him extremely.' Likewise you will find that in speaking of the bladder the Empiricist says: 'when the bladder is hard, and painful as well, this is a serious thing at any time, but it is most tormenting when combined with fever.' On his being asked for the reason, he produces a partial cause, and says: 'for in the pains arising in the bladder there is such severity that he suffers torments, and in addition to this the sick person is prone to be constipated when attacked by this disease.' The Dogmatist in a case of this kind will inquire into the functions and nature of the organ, and frames his statement as to the cause of this in accordance with these inquiries.

138

You will find, too, that the supporter of 'memory and observation' says: 'if a patient is found uncovering his feet—his feet not being very warm—and if he throws about his hands and feet, and puts them down aimlessly, this is a bad sign.' Now were he to be asked for the reason of this, he would say: 'Because this points to nervous irritation'. But the Dogmatist, on the other hand, would again commit himself to lengthy babble and useless theories, because he is not satisfied with plain observation, but must needs inquire into the substance and nature of the disease. Now, if you consider the question asked about a person who suffers from sleeplessness, what is the reason why insomnia and perpetual sleeplessness become so serious and severe that one is unable to sleep

either by night or by day—you will find that the Dogmatist sets to work
to consider the nature of sleeping and waking, and to find out what happens to the pneuma within the body so that it is affected by each of these
things. But you will find that the supporter of memory and observation in
saying: 'if one cannot sleep either by day or by night, it is a very bad sign'
makes an obvious thing the cause and says: 'because this man's sleeplessness arises either from pain and fatigue, or is a sign that he is suffering
from phrenitis'. Since this is how matters stand, it is perfectly clear and
139   obvious that a difference exists between each logos and conclusion used
by the Dogmatists, and the logos and conclusion known as epilogismos,
which is universally used by everybody, namely that epilogismos seeks
the guidance of visible things—and it is from those that it seeks confirma-
tion of its truth and rightness—whereas the conclusion called analogismos, avoids visible things and arrives at an invisible foundation and root,
which owing to its invisibility is peculiar to some people and not shared
by others, namely the elements and functions. For if the dogmatic physician wishes to explain the cause of sleep or fever, or the burning inflammation arising from the blood, or pleurisy or phrenitis, or indeed any of
those effects caused by nature or of the ailments arising from opposition
to it, then since he has received many diverse views on the matter he
must inevitably discover some special view of his own out of this diversity of views which does not command universal acceptance, nor conform to the method known as epilogismos. This is the reason why those
who do not accept his conclusion and do not agree with him upon it are
very numerous.

Chapter XXVI

Since matters are thus, Erasistratos is put to shame, and is discovered to
be mocking at himself, not at us, and to be leading himself, not us, into
error by telling of the man who poured hot water into a vessel and laid it
upon the affected part, so that it might be in contact with this part and
cover the place of the fold(?) (the inner part of the pubes?), with the
object of curing retention of the urine. For if knowledge of the three
kinds of vessels—i.e. of arteries and veins and sinews—point to this
method of therapy, and knowledge that the substances which flow in
those vessels remain unmixed, as well as knowledge of the views resulting again from these, by Zeus (la-^{c}amrī), he has every right to boast and
be proud of himself. But if another method and another argument points
to this kind of therapy, I do not think you will maintain that the manner

of this argument and this method is the inference from the visible to the invisible which is known as analogismos. For according to your way of thinking, no other argument and no other conclusion of this kind can be correct except your own argument and conclusion. Should it be discovered, however, by an argument and a conclusion after the manner of the conclusion from the visible to the visible, known as epilogismos, then it is, in the view of the Empiricists and mankind generally, something that is universal, comprising you and other people. Pray tell me, who is ignorant of the fact that something hot does not stimulate and set in motion every evacuation. Or who, think you, does not know that taking a hot bath sets in motion the evacuations of waste substances, and that we, if we wish to urinate, press the place of the inner part of the pubes(?)? But if he only equivocates and takes as his measure evident things, which are perceived by the eyes and are known to all people, what manner of conclusion from the visible to the invisible is there here, if this is a conclusion from the visible to the invisible? But as we do not deny this nor reject it, we too will call it two conclusions from the visible to the invisible, for I am not one of those who would dispute with you simply for the sake of a name.

Again the Dogmatist says: one of the advantages of the logos is that the instrument known as the catheter—it is (the instrument) which assists the passing of urine—was discovered by its means. But we would say, when we hear him maintaining a different opinion or (find him) holding a different view than this: whose arrant stupidity, think you, would go to such lengths as to inquire as to who invented and made this instrument, a man or an ass? Now since matters stand thus surely you will not choose this method but if you have confidence in yourself and believe yourself to be wise pray explain to us, then, how this instrument known as a catheter was discovered by conclusion from the visible to the invisible, and the victory is yours. I know, however, that you will not give us this explanation because you cannot prove it to have been discovered through knowledge concerning atoms and pores, nor by theories on the mixture, nor the disjunction and conjunction of substances, nor by any other logos of the Dogmatists. Should you, then, say: when I studied the shape of the interior of the bladder my keen powers of perception enabled me to construct this instrument whose shape resembles that of the bladder, we would answer: 'can it be thought of anyone of the Empiricists that he is ignorant of the shapes of members of the body, or that anyone of them avoids anatomy and rejects it, inasmuch as by its means knowledge of the shapes of the organs of the body and their place in the body cannot be discovered?' I, for my part, do not reject this, nor refuse to affirm it, but I do reject and refuse to affirm the statement of one who claims to

140

141

discover the natural functions and natural kinds by means of anatomy.
As for you, if you are really capable of instructing us on this point, as to
how this instrument, known as a catheter, was discovered, pray speak.
For we should like to be instructed by you, and shall delight in it after the
thing by which you assert it to have been discovered is something the
knowledge of which is shared by us and you and all the other Dogmatists. If, however, it is something asserted by you alone, then no. If you
do this, then you extol the conclusion from the visible to the visible
which is known as epilogismos, because this is something common to
you who use the logos, and to us who apply observation and memory,
and also to all other people. And when I bring forward all the things
which you Dogmatists declare have been discovered by conclusion from
the visible to the invisible and show that their discovery is made by conclusion from the visible to the visible, I carry my opinion to the extreme
and do not achieve my intentions, but in what we have brought forward
there is enough to make known all that we have not mentioned. In short,
when you do not say that the instrument was discovered by understanding the elements, nor by knowledge of the functions, nor by what has
already been said concerning diseases and causes, then this is the argument of one who makes use of the conclusion from the visible to the visible which is known as epilogismos.

Now leave this and take what remains of their theory on the phrenet-
ics, in which cases, they say, blood-letting must not be used because the
atoms are in the pores of the cerebral membranes. Reflect, now, if we
must not of necessity contradict their argument, since it is one known by
him who advances it to be after the manner of the conclusion from the
visible to the invisible, since it sets forth things which are not visible (and
you will find amongst the Dogmatists another who does not say this).
Thus it happens that this is something which you, Asclepiades, alone
profess. When you say: 'I saw in Parion that the condition of a man
attacked by phrenitis became worse on the application of blood-letting',
my answer is: 'I do not know if the opinion you express is correct; I do
know, however, that the source of your argument and its sequence is
after the manner of the argument that draws conclusions from the visible
to the visible and is known as epilogismos; for you direct me to what is
apparent to the eye by experiment and lead me to a matter most easily
understood and grasped with little difficulty by one who goes to these
lands and stays there until he can report on them. It would be incumbent
and most suitable for you not to do this, but rather to explain to us the
condition of the nature of these lands and their temperature, and to tell
us something about the bodily conditions of the inhabitants of these
lands, from what atoms and pores the bodies of the people who come to

142

these lands are constructed, and what the difference is between their
bodies and ours, so that your argument with me, and your address to me
may, at the moment, resemble the argument and the address of
Asclepiades. If, however, you should tell me only of such things as are
uttered by a man in the street, you would then say nothing suitable for
men of quality, and would give us nothing that resembles your two
requirements, but you would only be setting forth the information of the
lower and less intelligent class of the inhabitants of that country. Therefore, since this is the case, what you have discovered and elicited concerning the elements is vain and useless to you. Your boasts, too, about
atoms and pores are in vain, for when you set out for a certain city you
found yourself without a logos, because you left your logos in your
wretched papers at home fearing to have them with you in your travel
and transported with you in the ship, not being sure that the ship might
not be wrecked and yourself be drowned. You thus took refuge in experience, although you in particular despised and opposed Empiricism on
the ground that nothing could be discovered by its means. In this you
resemble the boastful Asclepiades in his lust for praise and the spread of   143
his fame, just because an old woman, one of the inhabitants of Parion,
was able to use her intelligence and memory in observing what goes on
there.'

You may think perhaps in listening to my argument and in reflection
thereon, that Asclepiades alone falls into such absurdities, and that the
other Dogmatists are perfectly reasonable. This, however, is not the case,
but rather that Asclepiades babbles and indulges in meaningless talk in a
measure for exceeding that of all the others. But the others say many
things resembling his. Should you wish to be assured of this, then see
how Erasistratos is not ashamed to put down in his book something quite
trivial and which, had it belonged to the more weighty views which have
been formulated and made accessible, would have furnished an explanation as to how the burning inflammation arising from the blood has its
origin. For he brings forward ridiculous and worthless arguments, adopting and arguing from many things concerning which there is no universal
unanimity, and neglecting many other convincing matters which contradict and confute and reject them, and the number of these is larger than
the number of things which justify and support them. And these are the
three kinds of vessels, and the substances which separate on the opening
of the entrance of one of the vessels into the other, and the falling of the
blood from the veins into the arteries, and the escaping and the dispersal
of the blood. But when he proceeds without reflection to supposition and   144
imagination on the matter in hand, he is a man who has a knowledge of
the causes of this disease, and has recourse to his own counsel in regard

to the therapy of the abscess of the throat. Just see what he says: 'the pills known as Andron-pills were not available, so I shall use the juice of brambles (mulberries) in their place.' Now the very fact of his using this juice instead of those pills makes it evident that he did so only because of its similarity to the remedies for constipation. Since this is the case, where then is his argument concerning natural functions, and his babble about the flowing of blood and its course from one vessel into the other, its escape and dispersal? But he is silent and refuses to answer. All the same, however, he never ceases producing something superfluous and presenting this, his own decision, as a doctrine to mankind. If you do no more, Erasistratos, than a man does who affirms the conclusion from the visible to the visible, then your efforts, and our efforts along with you, over the absurdities you have advanced in all these matters, have come to nothing, since they were things most necessary to us but have turned out useless. Now this very Erasistratos, the strong and powerful researcher into the nature of things, the wise in all things, is found to possess no superior virtue on entering the domain of therapy, and to be no better qualified than the Empiricists, employing as he does transferences from one thing to another similar to it. And this is a proceeding which is empirical(?) in all its forms. Moreover(?), we are most grateful to Andron for having discovered these pills, by reason of which Erasistratos was saved from disgracing himself and from finding himself at a loss at a time of need and exigency, although this Andron was one of the Empiricists. Should we, however, also include him amongst the Dogmatists, he nevertheless does not belong to those who share Erasistratos' views and affirm his opinion. It is probable that not even in sleep, far less in his waking hours, did he ever hear of the 'pouring of the blood into the veins', or of its 'flux from the veins into the arteries, and its escape into the veins and dispersal there'. Now if this should be the case, then these pills were not discovered by Erasistratos' theory, nor was it this same theory of his that transmitted what has been transmitted, but all this is due to the method of concluding from the visible to the visible, that is to the epilogismos, which is universal and common to all men.

145

CHAPTER XXVII

Now since this is the case, why are you so boastful, Erasistratos, praising yourself when you bring us nothing that you have yourself discovered? What you assert and describe is likely to prove on investigation to be something ignorant and crude, for you do but confuse and deceive people by your contradictory and equivocal way of arguing and by declaring: the logos discovered (the case of) the phrenetic to be uniform. When he speaks thus, we answer and say: what kind of logos is this? The logos of Erasistratos who operates with three kinds of vessels, or the logos of Asclepiades who operates with atoms and pores? Further, the circumstance that (the case of) the phrenetic is not found to be uniform is evident to everybody, in view of the fact that the mixtures and humours which are in our bodies are four or three or innumerable. Pray tell us by what theory this has been discovered, and we shall gladly listen to what you say. Perhaps you are doing violence to us and rejecting the authorities or attacking those who in no way deserve it only because it is incumbent on you, seeing that we do not find the (case of the) phrenetic uniform by virtue of reasoning from the visible to the invisible, to hate it and reject it on the ground that it is useless. You will then cease from giving that one the preference, and will assign blame to that which you ought to praise, if in your opinion also the knowledge that the (case of the) phrenetic is uniform is useful and confirmed by experience, and this were something the discovery of which is accomplished by the universal conclusion common to all men, whose method is the method of reasoning from the visible to the visible, which is called epilogismos, whereas the conclusion used by the Dogmatist could not accomplish this. Thus it is necessary for you to accept and recognize as sufficient the logos which is able to discover something of what ought to be discovered, and to reject and contradict the false logos.

CHAPTER XXVIII   146

And if you say that the symptoms are numberless, we would answer: we find that you yourself have stated them as though they were finite in your writings. Again, the theory of their finiteness is more binding on you than on me, since you used to consider them to be opposed to the natural functions which are not infinite. However, if you are able and willing, pray explain about them to me, not that they are infinite—for it is obvious that this is one of the things you cannot explain—and not that they are finite and very numerous—for this, too, is not possible—but rather tell me that there are only 100, and the victory is yours. Further, if you say that the possibilities of changing the order of their arrangement and sequence are infinite, we would answer you thus: what are the symptoms whose change of order and sequence you claim to be infinite? Were you to say that this applies to the symptoms which of necessity conform with (the course of) a disease, you would be in obvious difficulties, for in the case of one who is born with a certain disease and whose disease grows with him and reaches a climax with him, then turns, abates, and is dissolved with him, the birth, growth, maturity, and dissolution of both being simultaneous, it cannot be said that there are changes of sequence or priority or posteriority. Now were you to say that this applies to the symptoms which precede the disease or follow it, or appear at a later date, there would be nothing in this at all prejudicial to Empiricism, although, according to your way of thinking, these symptoms also would have a certain arrangement and necessary sequence. For you say: 'burning fever inflames the cerebral membranes, and it results from this that the atoms make their way to the 'finely divided thing', or those of them which do so become extremely fast and violent in motion all at once; this is followed by a stoppage of the atoms in the pores, which causes the disease known as phrenitis. Thereupon what lies beneath the cartilages spreads upwards, being attracted by the 'finely divided thing'(to leptomeres).' Now when the very numerous atoms rise and rub against the resisting parts, they are repelled. After this they return to the roomy parts which are capable of absorbing them, and for this reason the belly is loosened. Since this is the case, it is therefore necessary for the origin of the burning fever and its accompanying symptoms to come first, after which phrenitis follows, then comes the upward attraction of the regions of the cartilages and the phrenitis is followed by the loosening of the belly. These are things which, according to your view, must be thus, and not otherwise, although even if these things were not so, the symptoms whose appearance precedes the appearance of phrenitis, whatever and how many they may be, would point to the onset of phrenitis—whether they appear alone or combined with others, or whether their arrangement and sequence is disturbed, as for instance rough and coarse replies from a man of mild temper and good manners, or wakefulness, nervous sleep, pain in the muscles, noise in the ears, a fixed stare and twitching of the eyes. Now consider whether one can tell which of these and similar signs do not point to phrenitis, when they precede its outbreak. For my part, I would call this an impossibility, since if any one of them or more than one or all of them together appear—even if some appear first, and others are retarded—they are all symptoms pointing to phrenitis. But it is not possible for change in the arrangement and sequence of symptoms to occur in the case of symptoms which are preceded by something else, and this applies equally to the symptoms which follow.

147

Chapter XXIX

Now let us leave this subject and devote our attention to those things which one calls salient causes. We for our part have learned by observation the methods of treatment which we have committed to memory, according to what happens immediately before the outbreak of the disease, on the ground that this is a part of the whole conjunction and present interrelation of the symptoms. But the Dogmatists do not assert this at all, rather do they say: in accordance with the condition of the body resulting from the antecedent regimen, it might happen at the present moment to be affected by sunburn, for example, in the same way that it would be affected by the disease.

Since we, however, have committed to memory in this regimen also a therapy peculiar to it, we cure him by a method different from that which we recollect in connexion with someone suffering from an unpleasant rash, or who constantly eats hot and burning things—not by recollecting the case of one who suffers from a swollen belly and repletion and is at the same time unable to get rid of vitiated matter in his body by natural methods. In the case of a man, therefore, who employs a regimen incrassative to the humours, we bear in mind a therapy which is not the therapy we recollect in the case of a man who keeps to an attenuating regimen which emaciates the body. Likewise when a man is attacked simultaneously by a disease of the stomach and a pleurisy, we cure each of his diseases by means of the therapy reserved particularly for them in our memories, without their simultaneous conjunction having in any way put us to inconvenience. Further, if there is a possibility of the two therapies clashing, we turn our attention to the more severe and threatening of the two diseases. Thus do we deal with the things which are called salient causes.

Now with respect to the symptoms which are connected with recovery, they necessarily follow the symptoms connected with the disease, and in them there is no change of order and sequence. Were this even the case it would not injuriously affect the method of therapy at all. For example flushed cheeks, loss of hair, bent nails, and hot finger-tips are symptoms which follow the disease known as consumption. But reflect if these symptoms originate simultaneously, what change of sequence can there be? And if one of them comes first, and the others follows, what disadvantage arises therefrom for one who bears in mind the things which are beneficial to a patient suffering from this disease?

If you would like now to hear my opinion on the symptoms which are generated and appear later, then listen. I say that whichsoever of these symptoms is malignant and bad surely points to something bad, whether it be isolated, or whether it appears along with another symptom, or whether all the symptoms appear simultaneously, or whether one follows the other. And if any is good, it points to the reverse. If you should then answer: but when the disease known as 'loss of memory (lethargia)' is the disease following phrenitis, then it is bad, and if it is the disease which precedes it, then it is good, we would answer you thus: surely if a man applies his mind to these matters and recollects that things are thus, he can grasp it by the method of reasoning from the visible to the visible known as epilogismos. I say: if the change and transformation of a disease is in the direction of another more serious disease, or if the strength of the sick person has previously diminished, his condition must of necessity become worse. And if the change and transformation of the disease is in the direction of another less serious and less dangerous disease, the condition of the sick man will improve. This is the case, I am sure, with regard to lethargy: since this complaint belongs to those diseases that are more serious than convulsions, it is better if it changes into convulsions, and worse if it appears after convulsions. A similar case is that of 'acidity of the intestines'. For there is no one who does not know that the 'acid intestine' is less serious than the disease known as 'slipping of the intestines'. Since this is the case, there is no need to reason to the invisible with the help of the visible in order to diagnose the condition and inform ourselves that should the disease known as 'slipping of the intestines' turn into 'acid intestines', it is better and more favourable than its occurrence after 'acid intestines'. For this is something we are constantly meeting with, namely, that the change of diseases and their transformation into more serious complaints, is a graver and more difficult matter, and that their turning into less serious diseases is a more simple matter. Reasoning to the visible with the help of the visible, being the method known as epilogismos, is sufficient to discover this, and experience also suffices for the instruction of men concerning it. Here too we have no need at all for disquisition on the natural faculties.

Chapter XXX

Now should you say that change in the order and sequence of things used in healing is something infinite, we would answer you thus: In no way whatsoever does this either belong to our argument, since the total sum of the symptoms when they combine together always requires a single definite method of healing, and each single one of the symptoms which succeed these has its specific treatment, as experience has shown.

Again, we have learned by experience that we must start with evacuation of waste substances and then apply bandages. Further, experience teaches us that every kind of violent motion and bathing after food is not good. I am also of opinion that you will continue to postulate (reasons for) all such things as these and put them in the place of experience. For if you ask one another for the reason why it is not good to have a bath after food, and then each one of you adduces a cause different to that of the other, you will reach the conclusion that the one amongst you who tells the cause of it relates it only as an afterthought, having in fact learned the matter itself from experience. Now just as we have learned from experience this change in the things which we used in healing, I should have liked to learn from your school seven examples of the changes of things used in healing, but not to listen to you merely floundering and postulating things you have never seen. I expect you will say that change up to two or three times is possible and serviceable, but beyond that no advantage is to be gained. Or if anyone were able to explain to me a change of this kind, for the consideration of which the logos would suffice, but not experience, I should be delighted and grateful to learn it from him. But the case here is the same as in all other cases; that is to say, those things exist whose existence is only claimed and asserted, but not things which can be demonstrated by proofs.

If you wish to recognize the truth of this, consider the argument which you use to us, that we go wrong because we do not make a close study of every single thing with the help of the logos as you do. And when you change the arrangement and sequence of a thing whatever it may be, without knowing this chapter of medicine, so that what appeared irregularly becomes frequent, and what was frequent becomes constant, we should say of this too that if the change is something that can be registered by the memory then we shall accept it, and if it belongs to that which is not registered by observation and memory, then it is something far beyond the faculties of men, unattainable and impossible for them. But I presume that you will guarantee your knowledge of this, and assert   151
your claims to possess this knowledge, with complete confidence in yourselves, but without producing a single proof. Were this not so, the necessary consequence here too would be that one of you should practise medicine well and properly, but no one else among you who adopts the theoretical method should be able to do so. But if you should say to me: 'you can never learn to distinguish the excellent and praiseworthy thing which leads to a good end from the blameworthy thing which leads to a bad end', I should answer: 'even if we have not retained in our memories every single one of those things that produce a good or a bad effect in our bodies, your argument is nevertheless a plain falsehood.'

Were you now to say to us: 'why then do you not use your intelligence and search out and remember if your patient should have happened to sleep, or to speak, or what garments he was wearing?' we should answer: 'once again with these arguments of yours you but accuse yourself, not us. For we who adopt the method of memorizing and recollecting the things that happen make a practice of memorizing and recollecting those things amongst them from which there has occurred in the majority of cases obvious harm or benefit to an appreciable degree. But as for the other things, we do not trouble about them, nor concern ourselves with them, since the memory holds only those things which are of frequent occurrence. As for you, since you are convinced that our bodies undergo some kind of a change by reason of things one sees, to say nothing of other things, you have forbidden red colours to those who spit blood and yellow colours to sufferers from jaundice. For if you in questioning each one of your patients omit to ask about the colour of the garment he wore, in your efforts to learn something of the bodily condition of the sick man, your omission to do so is an act of remissness on your part and neglect of what is necessary. The same thing applies to asking whether someone has been walking with the sick person, or whether another has dined with him, or another slept with him; to one who thinks that bodies acquire some disordering influence from the material substances which approach them, it cannot be right to ignore them. If this then is the case, one can see that I, as an Empiricist, am in every way free from blame in giving no attention to such things, for I am a man who attends only to what can be perceived by the senses, recognizing nothing except that which can be ascertained by the senses alone with the help of observation and retention in the memory, and not going beyond this to any other theoretical construction. Therefore whatever I have stored up in memory as doing harm or good to an appreciable degree in themselves, and perceptible by sense, I affirm the advantage which is derived therefrom. But with respect to the things which perhaps are beneficial or harmful in some way or other, but whose benefit or injury cannot be perceived by the senses and retained in the memory, I refuse to recognize them, not because, if I were to recognize them, the knowledge of them would harm me, but because my observation and recollection do not reach as far as all this.

It is true that I ponder over many other things that you assert, as well as many things of the same sort which I find the old authority of our grandfathers' days repeatedly enjoins one who seeks a cure to avoid, such as forbidding a seeker after healing to shake hands with another person, or to dine with him, or to sleep with him, or wear such and such garments, or go to such and such a place, or to sleep in an upper or lower

152

room, and think it possible that these things too may have some effect. But that I think about and ponder over this is not an admission that I know anything of this kind.

It is likely that the same thing happens to me which often happens to others, namely, that I fail to attain my object and make mistakes in my medical practice, and do not always act correctly, since my knowledge is not true knowledge based on full investigation of the whole of mankind, but knowledge acquired at haphazard and that falls short of the truth. As for you, if you also say that you are baffled in these matters and fall short of attaining the truth in regard to them, you prove the case against yourself. If you should say, however, you are not baffled, then pray tell us   153 why you fail to attain your object, since it is incumbent on you, in virtue of your self-advertised claim to possess knowledge of the paltry things even of this degree of minuteness, that you should always be correct and successful and reach your goal, as far as it is humanly possible.

CHAPTER XXXI

For my part, I should like to make you understand in the fewest possible words that Empiricism suffices to discover everything used in healing. If it be the case that one who inquires into the natures of things cannot practise medicine properly without making use of experience, and if one who used experience alone practised medicine with such success as to become a recognized authority without requiring to use the method of reasoning from the visible to the invisible known as analogismos, and if one who has combined these two methods and applied them has made no change for the better in any chapter of medical science, then it is obvious that the method of reasoning from the visible to the invisible, the analogismos, does not suffice for the discovery of things useful for purposes of healing, neither if it is isolated, nor if it is supported by anything else. Now so that I can once and for all bridle you and put a muzzle on your lips, making you feel that you are cornered with no means of escape, I am prepared to concede that the method of reasoning from the visible to the invisible, known as analogismos, can discover everything. I shall then follow this up by proving that we have no need of it at this time for any useful purpose.

Therefore I would say: your argument is as follows: 'when I know a thing thoroughly and hold it for certain in virtue of the things perceptible to the eye to which I assign the part of signs from which I draw this inference, I proceed to elicit other invisible things by its means, and I reach my conclusion on the things which I shall use for treatment of the disease by inference from those invisible matters which I discovered with the help of those perceptible to the eye.' To this I reply: 'I have no intention of going beyond these reasonable things, and I admit their validity and accept your own assertion that if these signs are present, the method of healing cannot be other than the same correct method; and I shall not fall short of anything attained by you who have allowed the validity of eliciting matters of medicine from the whole (field of) medicine. For example, you do not deny that when a man is young and is attacked by pleurisy and his pulse is strong, blood-letting is necessary in his case.' If you should say that not one of the Empiricists knows the reason whether it is this or that, but that the Dogmatists know it, then we would say: 'you have no advantage over us in being able to effect better cures than we can. If this is not the case, pray prove it to us. For in our opinion it is not impossible for some young people whose pulses are strong to derive benefit from blood-letting, but there is nothing beyond that which compels us to inquire into the cause of their deriving benefit from blood-letting. But you, who are able to tell us the reasons for the usefulness of things used in healing, most assuredly utter greater absurdities and talk far more foolishly than we do, and withal you are of no greater use to the sick than we. However, we shall gracefully concede that you have discovered and learned by means of the logos why it is necessary to apply blood-letting to the man attacked by this disease. And we would say: 'We for our part do not know the logos and have no idea what it is, while he, on the other hand, is able to make use of what he has discovered and learned'. But now consider in what way you have an advantage over us at the moment in the application of things used in healing. I say: You have no advantage over us at all, as the things themselves clearly and unequivocally declare.

So since this is the case, although you have been indulgently conceded that everything used in healing has only been discovered by reasoning from the visible to the invisible, by the method known as analogismos, when it comes to practical handling of the means of healing at this time, you are not a whit better than we.

(To sum up) in our prior argument we demonstrated that experience suffices to discover the things used in healing. As for this argument which closes the whole discussion, it is an argument that speedily puts an end to your absurdities and prevents you from uttering further inanities. For it conceded to you that the sum of everything used in healing was discovered by the logos alone, and then demonstrated that we do not require it at all at this time.

Index of the Persons Mentioned in the Texts

Acron   xxiv, 23
Aenesidemus   xxvi
Aeschrion   xxxi
Albinus   xii, xv, xvii, xxxiv
Alexander   xxxiv
Alexandros   66
Andron   98
Apuleius   xvii
Aristotle   xiii, xvii–xx, xxiv,
    xxviii, xxxiii–xxxiv, 44
Asclepiades   xxviii–xxx, 8, 23,
    43, 45, 49, 50, 51, 68, 70, 85,
    91, 92, 96, 97, 98, 99
Asclepius   xii

Boethius   xxxiii

Cassius   27
Chrysippus   44
Chrysippus Medicus   70
Cicero   xxxiii
Commodus   xii

Democritus   xx, 62, 73
Diocles   xxii, xxviii, 69
Diogenes Medicus   69

Diogenes Laertius   xxxiv
Diogenes of Sinope   85
Dioscurides   xiii
Dogmatists   4, 7–12, 15, 23–24,
    32–33, 36, 43, 45, 51, 52, 58,
    60, 68ff.

Empedocles   xxiv
Empiricists   ix–x, xii–xiii, xix,
    xxii–xxvi, xxviii–xxxiii,
    xxxv–xxxvi, 3–4, 7–13,
    15–16, 23–37, 41–45, 49–50,
    51, 52, 56, 57, 58, 60, 63,
    67ff.
Epicureans   xviii, xxviii–xxix
Erasistratus   xxii, xxiv, 8, 23, 65,
    68, 69, 70, 91, 94, 97, 98
Eudemus   xv

Gaius   xvii
Glaucias   xxvi, 43
Gorgias   xxiv

Heraclides of Tarentum   44
Herophilus   xxii, xxiv, xxviii,
    28, 70, 91

Hierocles 66

Hippocrates xiii, xv, xvii,
   xx–xxi, xxx–xxxi, 14, 17, 36,
   42–44, 63, 69, 70, 85, 91

Lucius Verus xii

Marcus Aurelius xii

Menodotus x, xxvi, xxix, 25,
   27, 34–36, 42–44, 51

Methodists ix–x, xxix–xxxii,
   xxxvi, 10–13, 20, 52

Peripatetics xii, xv, xvii–xvii,
   xxviii, xxxiv

Petron 70

Philinus xxvi, 23

Philotimus 69

Plato xii, xv, xvii–xx, xxiii–xxv,
   xxviii, xxxiv, xxxvi, 31, 57

Pleistonicus 65

Polus xxiii–xxiv

Praxagoras xxii, 23, 69, 70, 85,
   91

Pyrrho x, xxvi, 42–43

Quintilian xxxiii

Rationalists ix–x, xii, xxii–xxiii,
   xxv, xxvii–xxxiii, 3–4, 6, 8,
   49 ff.

Serapion 23, 27, 42–43, 51

Severus 43–44

Sextus Empiricus x, xxvi, xxviii

Socrates xxiii

Soranus xiii, xxxi

Stoics xii, xvii–xix, xxviii,
   xxxiii–xxxiv

Themison xxix

Theodas xxvi, 26–29, 45

Theodosius 51

Thessalus xxix–xxxi, 11

Timon 23, 42

Index of the Subjects Mentioned in the Texts

analogism   9, 33, 36, 62, 64, 66, 71, 88–89, 90, 91–93, 94, 95
antecedent causes   7–8, 13–15
autopsia   xxvi, 4, 25

cause   xx–xxii, xxviii–xxx, 5–7, 9–10, 12–14, 16, 18–20, 28–30, 32, 55, 68, 69, 70, 78, 93, 94
coinvadentia   31
communities   xxx, 10–11, 16, 19–20
conservation   26
constitutive parts of medicine   27–29

definition   xvi, 9, 11, 32–33
degrees of expectation   37–38, 72
description   xxv, 33, 35
disagreement between theories   xxv–xxvi, xxxii, 10, 16–17, 29, 33, 45
distinction   xvi, xxv, 17, 25, 29, 31–32, 35

epilogism   xxiii, 9, 33, 36, 44, 88–89, 91–93, 96, 98, 102

experience   ix, xi, xiii, xxi–xxxiii, 3–5, 8, 14, 23–29, 31, 34–40, 43, 45, 49, 57, 58, 60, 64, 66, 69, 102, 103, 106
extemporary experience   4, 24–25

history   x, xv, xix, xxvii–xxviii, 5, 25–29, 33–39, 57

imitative experience   24–25
incidental experience   24
incomprehension   9
indication   xix, 2, 6–7, 9–11, 13, 24, 36–37
invention   xxxiv, 5, 8, 49, 60, 63, 95, 105–106

judgment of history   35–39

language   9, 28, 41
logic   xiv, xvi–xviii, xxiii, xxvii–xxviii, xxxiii–xxxiv, 9, 17, 33, 37, 44–45, 58

memory   4, 26–27, 31, 33, 44, 63, 103, 104

observation   xiv, xxi–xxii,
    xxvi–xxvii, xxx, xxxii–xxxiii,
    3–5, 7, 11, 25–27, 29, 31, 33,
    36, 41, 49 ff., 73
one's own perception   xix, xxvi,
    xxxii, 4–5, 16–17, 24–26,
    28–29, 33, 35–36, 44–45

parts of medicine   25–28
practice   xiv, xvii, xx–xxi,
    xxiii–xxv, xxvii–xxviii, xxx,
    xxxii, 10, 12, 14, 19, 26,
    33–36, 57
practiced experience   5, 24–25
practician   26, 34, 78, 79
practitioner   xx, xxv–xxvii, 34
procatarctic cause   xv, xxii, 52,
    101

reason   xix, xxii–xxiv, xxvi,
    xxviii–xxx, xxxii–xxxiii,
    3–5, 8, 14–17, 19, 24, 26,
    28–29, 33–34, 36–37, 43–45,
    49, 60, 63, 69, 74, 87, 95, 98

similarity   24, 26–27, 30, 37–38
sorites   25, 59, 74 ff., 81 ff.
symptom   xxix–xxx, 7, 16,
    29–30, 32, 55
syndrome   7, 30–32

theorem   xxvii, 4, 24–26, 42, 57
theory   ix, xiv, xviii–xxii, xxv,
    xxviii–xxxiii, 9, 17, 34, 44,
    67–68, 71, 80, 93, 98, 99,
    102–103, 104
transition to the similar   xxvii,
    5, 25–28, 36–37